4GVN

The powerful testimony
of ghetto preacher
Willy Ramos

Pacific Press® Publishing Association
Nampa, Idaho
Oshawa, Ontario, Canada
www.pacificpress.com

Cover design by Steve Lanto
Cover design resources supplied by the author
Cover photo by Tanya James
Inside design by Aaron Troia

Copyright © 2010 by Pacific Press® Publishing Association
Printed in the United States of America
All rights reserved

Additional copies of this book are available by calling toll-free 1-800-765-6955 or by visiting http://www.AdventistBookCenter.com.

ISBN 13: 978-0-8163-9303-9
ISBN 10: 0-8163-9303-6

10 11 12 13 14 • 5 4 3 2 1

MY TWO HEROES AND INSPIRATION TO WRITE

"I walk with trembling before God. I know not how to speak or trace with pen the large subject of the atoning sacrifice. I know not how to present subjects in the living power in which they stand before me. I tremble for fear lest I should belittle the great plan of salvation by cheap words."

Ellen G. White (*Selected Messages,* bk. 3, 115)

"By the grace of God I am what I am, and his grace to me was not without effect."

Apostle Paul (1 Corinthians 15:10)

DEDICATION

To my parents: Pedro and Adelaida Ramos. My superheroes!

Though we hardly ever had enough, you guys never gave up. Thank you for planting that same seed in me. I can't wait to see you guys enjoying heaven. Finally, you'll get what you guys so much deserve. I'm sorry for all the pain I've ever caused you guys. I owe "yous" my life! I love "yous"!

!Bendición!

IN MEMORY OF

Brian David Vega and to the family he left behind:
David, Sandy, JoJo, and Becky.
This book is for you.

ACKNOWLEDGMENTS

People will never forget movie characters like Bubba from *Forest Gump* or Apollo Creed from *Rocky*. I even remember the dog from *I Am Legend*. Some supporting actors are funnier or more memorable than the lead actor. Some may work harder as well.

I would love to take some time out to honor the supporting actors of this book. Thank you for what yous have done for me in my life. May God repay yous. (Drum rolls, please . . .) "And the award for Best Supporting Actor or Actress goes to . . .

"Pastor Sergio Torres (Master Yoda). Thank you for recommending me for the book *Changed*. You have been my agent, mentor, and friend from the beginning. May God bless you, always.

"Pastor Manny Cruz. You are a brother to me. I got your back 'til the end. Thank you for always putting your neck out and vouching for me. Love you, homie.

"Miguel Valdivia and Carlos Camacho. You guys are fearless. Thank you for believing in me.

"Elder Jerry D. Thomas. Thank you for believing in me

and for your patience! We did it! Thank you for helping me proclaim the name of our 'Messiah' (Cheap plug!), Christ Jesus!

"Pacific Press®. I'm so proud of this publishing house! First, *Changed,* now *4GVN!* Wow! I thank you for allowing the readers to hear a voice that's been crying from the wilderness a long time now. It's my honor and a privilege to partnership with you for God's glory and honor.

"Pastor Tony Avila. You still are my favorite singer! Thank you for believing I can do it.

"Richard Guerrero (O.G.). We're pocos pero locos, ¡carnal! Thank you for believing that God can use a street punk like me and for always sharing your pulpit.

"Pastor Leroy Chacon. You and Manny made me want to pursue higher learning. And because of that, I have my diploma! Next stop? The White House! (Hey, Obama did it!)

"Max Lucado. Thank you for the many laughs in this ugly world. (I pray I do the same for my readers.) Through God's Spirit, your books have touched me. I look forward in meeting you some day.

"The Ramos Family (Janet, Papo, Lily, Cuca) and my old crew: The Ultimate Force. (May we never forget where we came from.) You guys are the inspiration of most of my sermons. I love all of you. I pray that just like we had awesome memories in the hood, we will have even better ones in the new kingdom when God comes.

"Lynette: mi *Gatita.* But you're more than a supporting actress. You're my leading lady! Thank you for sharing me with the world. You are amazing. May we live happily ever after like in them fairy tale books. You deserve it. I love you with all my heart and soul! *Mua!!*

"And last, but certainly not least, I want to thank God. I am Your supporting actor. Thank You for loving me and putting up with me. Thank You for sending me Lynette and Christian. They complete me. I hope I make You proud. I look forward to bear-hugging You real soon. You are the MAN!"

TABLE OF CONTENTS

JUST ADD WATER

"Your family is so poor, when I went to your apartment and stepped on a cigarette, your dad shouted out, 'Hey, who turned off the heater?!' " I used to hear jokes like that all the time. I grew up in poverty. In fact, we weren't POOR, we were PO'! Somebody stoled the last two letters from the word! That's how grimy my neighborhood was!

My pops worked for $3.35 an hour to sustain seven of us. The way we eat, I honestly don't know how he did it! (Three of us needed gastric bypass surgeries!)

We were so poor, we only had white rice to eat at times. No gandules, just arroz! My brother and I would go to Burger King to steal ketchup packets to mix it in the rice. (Some of you guys are smiling right now, cause you still do it!)

When we didn't have laundry detergent, we would use Joy dish detergent that we bought at the dollar store for ninety-nine cents.

The worst was when it was time to take a bath. My mother always had my sisters go first. Then my brother, the bully/jacker (who once SOLD me his collection of Star Wars action figures when he outgrew them!), would skip in front of me in the line and leave me for last. So by the time I took a bath, all the shampoo was gone! Between my sisters' Pocahontas hairdos—not to mention the hair on their armpits—(Ha! Just kidding!) and my brother's Steven Seagal mullet, they had enough hair to rival Chewbacca! And at the time, I had an afro! Somebody once called me Fat Albert! "Hey, hey, hey!"

Now what do I do? Ain't no shampoo left! Can't use soap. Last time I did that I got dandruff the size of snowballs. So there I'd be, naked with an empty shampoo bottle, screaming out to my mom for answers. (Spanish mothers are funny. Almost always, they're short little fat ladies who smell like sofrito, but have the wisdom of King Solomon. They have an old school remedy for everything. Usually, it's Ben-Gay!) My moms would tell me, "Take the shampoo bottle, twist off the cap, and add some water to mix it with the little bit of shampoo that's still left. Then close the cap back up and shake it like a Polaroid picture."

Then magic happens. Now my mom ain't no David Copperfield, but what happens when I add water to the little bit of shampoo that's left can land her a job with Ringling Brothers! I don't know how, but the added water makes the shampoo last for two more whole weeks! Long enough until my dad gets paid and buys another bottle.

Now the shampoo analogy applies to all of us. Some of yous are reading this book on empty. You have no relationship with Jesus. You hardly go to church anymore. And you never read the Bible.

Well, let me give you a little advice. Why not try adding Water? The Bible describes God as "Living Water."[1] So if you're walking around on "E," invite Jesus back into your life. Add some of that Living Water into your bottle and let Him shake you up. And who knows, after reading this book, you might have put sufficient enough Water to last you until the second coming of Christ!

> Water, Water, Pour on me /
> And wash me clean, wash me clean …
> Water, Water, to my soul /
> don't let me go, don't let me go, without
> . . . Water.
>
> —Ana Laura (Christian recording artist)

---

1. See Jeremiah 2:13.

Top Left: Back 'n' da days
Top Center: With kids singing "Jesus Luvz Me"
Top Right: Master Yoda, Sergio Torres
Right: My parents, my superheroes
Far Right: My other mentor, Richard Guerrero
Bottom Left: In the streets
Bottom Center: B4 & After
Bottom Right: Before

Help stop gang violence rally

Hulk Hogan

My brother, Papo

Jennifer Lopez

Al Pacino

Snoop

Kurt Angle

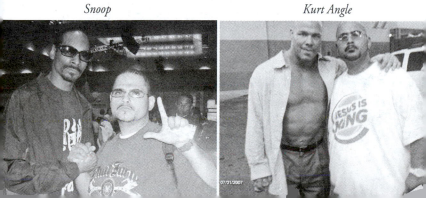

My baptism, April 24, 2000

My mentor, Pastor Manny Cru...

My 1st baptism

With wifey, Lynette, & son, Christian

My gatita

My sister Janet, Lily, & Cuca

Wedding day

CHAPTER ONE
$iNtRODUCtiON

I was there when my homeboy, Roland Martinez, killed a dude named Manny. I could've called the police. I didn't. I could've stopped him. Why didn't I? Maybe it was my loyalty to the mean streets or my fidelity to our street gang. Or maybe it was just my street knowledge kicking in, saying, "See no evil; hear no evil."

I didn't do anything. That Friday, I just froze. Or if I want to be real honest with you, I did do something. Something bad. I watched. I even held him down as Roland (Ro-Dawg) stabbed him four times.

"Yo, what you do?! Man, you killed him! You killed 90210!" I cried. But I was just as guilty.

We killed a rich white kid from the suburbs. He only wanted to be down. His only bad was wanting to hang out with thugs like us. I kinda liked the dude, to be honest, but Ro-Dawg didn't like him at all. He felt that the white boy should stay inside his MTV crib, surrounded by his white picket fence.

"We boyz-n-da hood! We from the PJs! Why he always trying to follow us, anyways? Who invited him?!"

Ro-Dawg was right. This dude was trying to be like us. He was a "wannabe." (Even though, when I think about it, he never partook in any of our sins. Go figure.) We dressed in Dickies; he had on the Hollister shirts. We wore Chuck Taylors; he wore expensive loafers that made him look like Sonny Crockett from *Miami Vice*. We had the jacked-up cars; he drove his daddy's BMW. He had it all. Clothes, Movado watches, cars, and a big house! But he still wanted to hang. Pretty soon, he started wearing Dickies and Converses just like us. He even talked street lingo.

One day we were at a house party where some girls were skipping school and everyone got wasted. I never smoked weed, but I was high off the contact. Plus, that day I drank eight, 32-ounce bottles of wine! That's 256 ounces of alcohol in my system! I was messed up. I couldn't think right. But we were all having "fun" when 90210 walked in.

"Who the hell invited Manny?" Ro-Dawg demanded angrily. Now Ro-Dawg was a lot more gangsta than me. He was a thug, like 2Pac. I'm the funny one, like the Fresh Prince of Bel-Air. He was drinking and smoking weed. If I was messed up, imagine what kind of shape he was in!

He was really wasted when he sucker-punched 90210.

Manny fell down and Ro-Dawg just kept punching him. That beatdown made UFC fighters look like Girl Scouts. Then some of my other homeboys jumped in as well. Not to defend 90210, but to help Ro-Dawg beat him down! Even the girls were spitting at him and slapping the dude in the face. Peer pressure made me do the same. After I whacked him like five times, I grabbed him from behind in a "full nelson" position, made famous by WWE wrestlers.

Then the knife came out. Everything was in slow motion after that.

Six members of our gang (The T.U.F.) got arrested that evening, including me. What did we do? We all looked spaced-out like zombies as they held us in a cell. No one said a word. Everything happened so fast. One of my other home-boys, Krusho, kept throwing up. But that was nothing new. Every Friday and Saturday night, after the clubs, he'd be drunk and would always end up bowing down to the white porcelain god—or as most of us know it, a toilet.

A guard came in to take us before a judge. "Don't we get one phone call?" I asked. But we didn't. Shackled together, we shuffled out to a courtroom and appeared before this old-looking dude dressed in a black Darth Vader robe.

This courtroom wasn't like those big rooms that you see on *Law & Order*. It was a small, cramped-up room that we almost didn't fit in. The judge shook his head and did something that shocked us all. He said, "You guys are free to go. Guards, unlock their chains. Now get out of here before I change my mind!"

"*Whaaat?* They're letting us go?" Unbelievable! Apparently, Manny's father didn't want to press charges. The state was seeking the death sentence, but the dead boy's pop said, "No one else has to die."

Usually, the state presses a murder charge regardless of what the family wants. But for some reason, this time they didn't. Ro-Dawg ran out that courtroom quicker than O. J.

Simpson after the jury pronounced him "Not guilty." I looked at Krusho, Rey-Rey, Joselito, and Casper and said, "Man, we need to start going to church." They all agreed.

As we got outside the courthouse, I saw Manny's father standing next to his Beemer. It was like he was waiting for me. I remember meeting the man before, even eating at his house. I was embarrassed. I couldn't look at his face. When he spoke to me, I worked up the nerve to look at him and could see that he was crying. He said, "Now, what are you going to do with the freedom I just gave you?"

Before I could answer him, my brother Papo pulled up to pick us up. We all jumped in the car faster than bank robbers fleeing a crime scene. That weekend, I visited my mom's church and gave my life to Christ.

Today, I am a youth evangelist. The kids call me "The Ghetto Preacher." I've been everywhere from Portland, Oregon, to Slovakia preaching the Word of God to everyone and anyone who will listen. I preach in churches, but not just there. I spread God's Word on street corners, in jailhouses, and at homeless shelters. In the words of Martin Luther King Jr., I'm "Free at last . . . Free at last! Thank God Almighty, I'm free at last!"

I still can't believe God can use a piece of junk like me. Measly ol' me? Once upon a crime, I was a thief with a gangsta mentality. I was also suicidal and homeless. A born loser.

But "the man behind the 8-ball" now preaches behind a pulpit. I am still a loser, though, to be honest. But I'm a loser of a different type. The Bible says "whoever loses his life for my sake will find it."[1]

The words of that boy's father still penetrate my ears and heart today. *"What are you going to do with the freedom I just gave you?"*

Me? I'm gonna help to change the world. Just like God changed a murderer like me.

What about you? What are you gonna do with the freedom God has given you? If I look closely at the people who were at that party that Friday, it wasn't just me and my homeboys. You were there also. Yeah, you! So was Billy Graham and Mother Teresa. So was Oprah and Al Pacino and Robert De Niro!

We're all murderers! You see, we're all guilty of killing a "rich boy" named Jesus of Nazareth, also known as Immanuel[2] or "Manny." He, who is a King, left His kingdom—heaven—(90210) to live in the barrio with us. He dressed like us, talked like us, and even became one of us. He just wanted to be loved by us and we killed Him. We stabbed Him three times and once on the side. Ro-Dawg and the Roman soldiers were not the only ones that stabbed Jesus—we stabbed Him too. And we held Him up on a cross. We're all guilty.

So we all deserve capital punishment. The Bible says, "The wages of sin is death."[3] But He forgives us. And His Father, who is also the Judge,[4] let us go free. Now I ask you again: What are you gonna do with the freedom God gave you?

---

1. Matthew 10:39.
2. Matthew 1:23.
3. Romans 6:23.
4. James 4:12.

CHAPTER TWO

FREE WILLY

I was filled with anger, so mad that I was crying like somebody died. I told my father that I hated him and wanted nothing to do with him anymore. I even did the unthinkable and cursed him out. I dropped so many curse words I sounded like one of these vulgar comedians or a gangsta rapper.

I was embarrassed, to be honest, as I thought of the words my mom once said to me: "That kind of language shows people how dumb you really are, because you cannot express yourself intelligently without cursing."

But I didn't care. Forget my father! "Forget this stupid life," I said to myself. I was so mad, I wanted to die. In fact, I decided to go home and kill myself. "I'm going to blow my brains out with the .38 Special my dad has hidden in the closet."

It was two in the morning after a long Sunday night and I had just asked God to prove His love for me. I was in front of a church across the street from my house, screaming at a cross. You see, I wasn't having a fight with my pop. I was having an argument with Jesus. I said, "Lord, if You don't give me a sign that You exist and that You love me, I'm going to shoot myself! Turn off one of these street lights or something!"

I gave Him ten seconds. It felt like an eternity. He didn't respond.

Just two days earlier, I was homeless. My mom had kicked me out of the house because of rap music. I had no job. I got fired for fighting. I got kicked out of school for the same reason. Even my girlfriend at that time dumped me. She said I disgusted her. I guess me—fat and in sweatpants—wasn't a pretty sight. I had lost everything. In fact, the only thing I couldn't lose was weight!

I felt hopeless and crippled.

It reminds me of a story I once read in the Bible. David was king of Israel at that time. His best friend, Jonathan, and Jonathan's dad had died at war, and Davey-boy remembers a pinky swear he did with John-John. They had sworn an oath to watch each other's backs and to always look after each other's families.[1] So one day when David was sitting on his throne, he asked, "Is there anyone still left of the house of Saul to whom I can show kindness for Jonathan's sake?" And this dude named Ziba said, "Yup. Johnny-boy had a crippled son who's still living." When David asked where he was, Ziba said, "He's in Lo Debar."[2]

Now I looked up the name "Lo Debar," and it has four different meanings: (1) Lacking something, (2) Not useful, (3) Nothing, and (4) No bread. The first three could mean crippled physically. But I think the fourth meaning is spiritual.

"No bread." I think the correct translation to that could be, "No Jesus." After all, didn't Jesus describe Himself as the Bread of Life?[3]

So check this out—this dude was not only crippled physically, I think he was crippled spiritually as well. He didn't have Jesus.

Worldly people often feel the same way. They feel a void in their lives that they try and fill with sex, drugs, or alcohol. They feel like they have no purpose, like they're of no importance.

What they need is Bread. What we all need is Jesus.

Now allow me to compare David with God for just a minute. Just like David sent for Jonathan's crippled son, God does the same thing, daily, from heaven. I believe God would say it like this: "Is there anybody still left from the house of Adam to whom I can show kindness for the sake of My Son, Jesus?"

You see, we are all crippled if we don't have Jesus. So I thank God for that question. Because that night, when I was screaming out for Jesus, I didn't hear Him, but He was calling out for me.

And today, though you can't hear it either, He's asking the Holy Spirit, "Is there anybody still left in New York, Chicago, Florida, or LA? How about in the projects, the suburbs, or the 'hotel, motel, Holiday Inn'?"

That night when I was down to nothing, God was up to something. When I couldn't hear Him, it was because He was busy preparing my comeback.

And Mephibosheth, Jonathan's crippled son, was about to live the comeback story of his own. He was brought before King David, and gave the king props by bowing down.[4] The dude couldn't even believe he was sent for by the king! He even degraded himself and said he was "a nobody," just a "dead dog."[5]

Pastor Gary James once told me in a phone conversation that he has a sermon about uplifting black men. He tells them that they should value themselves more because of what God did for them by offering the ultimate sacrifice to die in their stead. So, by calling each other names like the *N* word, or "dawg," contradicts what Jesus did for us on Calvary. He says that God made us rulers over all the animals on earth.[6] So why call each other names that keep us down, like a dog that walks on four legs?

When I heard that, I kind of changed the whole way I talked, and even thought. We shouldn't answer to what the world calls us, but by what God calls us. Ladies, that goes for you, as well. Don't answer if some dude calls you the *B* word unless that word is "beautiful."

One of my favorite authors affirms what Pastor Gary is talking about when she says, "The Lord is disappointed when His people place a low estimate upon themselves. He desires His chosen heritage to value themselves according to the price He has placed upon them. God wanted them, else He would not have sent His Son on such an expensive errand to redeem them."[7]

I started to change what I thought of myself as I got closer to God. I used to hate myself. I weighed 428 pounds, so I was always miserable. I didn't have love handles, I had hate handles! It's almost funny because I was born premature and only weighed four pounds when I came out. Not too many years later, somebody added two zeros behind that four!

Once I got kicked out of a plane because I was too big. Well, not while it was up in the air! But you can imagine how I felt. Sad. Embarrassed. Mad. I started to hate myself even more after that and I wanted to die.

And that was as a Christian! A breakthrough finally came when Pastor Manny Cruz and a lot of church members from New Mexico and Clermont, Florida, gave me a love offering so I could get the gastric bypass surgery. That surgery saved my life. I thank everybody who contributed even a penny to help me. One hundred and forty-something pounds lighter, I'm still preaching the Word like they ain't never heard! I owe you big time, guys! Pastor Tony Avila told me I should make "Ghetto Preacher" wallets, with my excess skin and sell it on eBay or Craigslist! Ha!

I am a walking miracle. Even though once upon a crime, I was a professional thief (I don't know how I used to fit through the windows of people's houses, but the Bible does say the devil also does miracles!), I've been sent for by God! And to be used by God for His honor and glory! My homie, Fernando Diez, once told me that I am "God's weapon of choice," when I'm behind the pulpit.

Me, who bit off a piece of somebody's cheek when I was losing a fight? Me, who hit a kid on the head with a baseball bat because he called me fat? Me, who would fight anybody and everybody who tried me or looked at me funny? God sent for me? Wow. I can't understand it. And I still don't get it. The boys in the hood are still confused and think it's some kind of mix-up. Because when I tell them, "God bless you," they ask me, "Why? I didn't sneeze!" It's hard for them to believe it. And it's hard for me too.

I once beat up an old lady for calling me a bum! Mike Tyson once said on *Oprah* that he didn't think God had created a person that could beat him when he was in the ring. That's exactly how I felt. Why am I telling you guys this? Because I was jacked up, yet God still sent for me!

It's time for you to get pumped up, as well. Because God wants to do the same for you too. Are you so far gone that you think God does not want anything to do with you? Are you renting an apartment in Lo Debar like Mephibosheth? Do you feel so messed up that you don't think God will answer your prayers? Have you called out to God and heard nothing but silence? If that's the case, smile! Rejoice. Your redemption is around the corner! You're gonna be alright!

I once heard a story about a barbershop owner in a small country town. He was the only barber there and had no competition at all. Which was a good thing because his family depended on that income to live. But then big business came to town and built a plaza right next to his shop. They set up a Starbucks, a Dunkin' Donuts, a movie theater, and . . . another barbershop!

The barbershop owner and his family were devastated at first. The new shop was taking all the business by putting up signs that read "$6.00 Haircuts." So in an act of desperation, he put up his own sign. It read, "I Fix $6.00 Haircuts!"

And that's exactly what Jesus does. He fixes $6.00 haircuts. Those of us that are tore up from the floor up. Just wait until God gets a hold of you!

Let Him. Stop resisting. Surrender.

Let me give you an analogy that might make you say, "Eww." My mother's family was so poor, she was forced to drop out of school in the second grade to babysit. So even now from time to time, she still does it. Once she was babysitting this little girl named Milta. While my mother was in the kitchen cooking, Milta would be watching television. But she would put her face so close to the television, you would swear she was making out with it. So my mom would scream at Milta to stop or threaten her that she'd go blind. I was working the night shift at the time, and I would sleep during the day. So every time Moms yelled at Milta, I would wake up scared, wondering, "Why is my mom screaming?"

One day I was fed up. My mom had just screamed at the little rug rat twice. So I got up from bed and tiptoed behind Milta as the *Pink Panther* tune played in the background. My plan was to scare her. She ended up scaring me.

When I crept up behind her, I saw her picking her little nose. *Eww,* I thought. *That's so gross.* Now, like a lot of kids, she wasn't sure what to do with what she found there. She looked at my mom to see if she was watching, but Mom was busy cooking. I was busy trying to come up with a plan to beat her with my flip-flops without getting caught. Then she did the unthinkable—something so gross she could have qualified for her own reality show. She put it back!

Some kids have no sense! I shouted, "Cochina, no!" I was so scared for her—I almost gave her CPR!

You know what? We do the same thing sometimes. And don't be a Speedy Gonzales to deny it. Because God sends for us, then He fixes us up. He removes the sins from our lives. And what do we do? We don't let God get rid of the sins for us. No, we put those sins back. I don't know who's worse, us or little Milta!

Allow Him to unlock those handcuffs that the devil has placed on your life. You can't escape by yourself. No defense attorney can get you out of this mess. Not even Johnnie Cochran. You need Jesus. Only He can free you.

Remember how big I used to be? Big like a whale? The little kids used to call me "Free Willy" when that movie came out. I would hide out for months until another movie made people forget that one. Then part two came out, and then part three. I was trying to reform and act right, so I couldn't beat those little bebe kids up. Instead, I became a hermit.

But you know what? Now I don't care. They can call me "Free Willy" all they like. Because I am free now. God has rescued me from myself and from a world full of sin.

Amen.

You want to know what happened to Mephibosheth or Mr. Meph, as I like to call him, when he went to the king's palace? The Bible says that after that he "ate at David's table like one of the king's sons."[8]

And we can too. For Jesus Himself said to "Go to the street corners and invite to the banquet **anyone** you find."[9]

---

1. 1 Samuel 20:17.
2. See 2 Samuel 9:1–4.
3. John 6:35.
4. 2 Samuel 9:6.
5. 2 Samuel 9:8.
6. Genesis 1:26.
7. Ellen G. White, *The Desire of Ages,* 668.
8. 2 Samuel 9:11.
9. Matthew 22:9; emphasis added.

CHAPTER THREE

JESUS IS MY CO-PILOT

(And I'm Flying Myself Straight to Hell! Mayday! Mayday!)

> There's two people living within my chest /
> One of them is evil, the other one is blessed;
> One of them I love, the other I hate /
> The one I feed will dominate!
>
> —Author unknown

"My name is Willy Ramos, and I'm an alcoholic." I'm told that's one of the first things you admit when you join Alcoholics Anonymous. Fortunately, I have never had to say that, even though I used to get drunk on wine, back in the days. The fact is, I haven't drank in almost a decade (Glory be to God!), not even as a Christian as some are accustomed to. (And accustomed to thinking that it's OK with God. Wink. Wink.)

But I'll tell you something that I am. I am—to quote the apostle Paul—I am "the chief of all sinners."[1] I have cursed at people, I have fought, I have looked at pornography, I have stolen, and I have lied. Now I'm not talking about before I was a Christian (even though everything I just named, I did in those days too!). But I've also done all those things from behind a pulpit. I could go on and on, but that would only give those "holier than thou" Christians an excuse to criticize me more.

But wait! Before you judge me or report me to the infamous "La Junta," let me remind you that not only did I just describe myself—and maybe you—I also described some of our Bible heroes that we admire so much. People like Abraham, David, Peter, and Paul.

Not long ago, I heard Steve Brown on a Christian radio station saying that he didn't have to look at the evening news or read the paper to remind himself that this world is messed up. All he had to do was look in the mirror. I feel the same. I disgust myself at times. And I'm a preacher; I should know better! "I do not understand what I do. For what I want to do, I do not do, but what I hate, I do. . . . But it is sin living in me that does it."[2]

Did you get that? We read the Bible too fast sometimes. The scripture is saying that sin lives in me! It's not an unwanted visitor or a wedding crasher. Paul is saying that sin comes inside your crib, takes off his stinky shoes, scratches himself, raids the refrigerator, and makes himself at home! He ain't a guest, he's a tenant! And if that's not bad enough, he doesn't pay rent, either! (I just described your teenagers, didn't I?)

When I was a new jack, I remember sitting at a red light and reading the bumper sticker of some woman's car that read, "Jesus Is My Co-Pilot." With the matchless love and zeal of a new believer, I smiled, honked my car horn, and gave her a thumbs-up that would've made Siskel, Ebert, and even The Fonz very proud.

That was ten years ago. I was real naïve. Today I wouldn't give her a thumbs-up—I would give her the finger! (Don't close the book up just yet, I'll explain in a few.) If Jesus is your Co-Pilot, you're flying yourself straight to hell! If He's not the pilot, we're heading for a major crash.

I read a recent article that reported that some pilots are allowed to fly even after failing their flight exam. Even after they got an F! Now that's stupid. But are we any smarter? We think that we have it all together sometimes. We start eating right, we give tithes and offerings, we keep the Sabbath day holy, then we start getting cocky. "Yo, I got this. I'm kinda straight right now, Lord. When I need Your help, I'll call You." We snatch the position that's rightfully His as Pilot and make Him our Co-Pilot.

That's why we keep messing up. Then sin sees how weak we are, signs a bootleg lease, and moves right on in. And some of us end up sleeping on the couch! You never see a bully pick on a jock or gangsta-looking kid and rob them of their lunch money, do you? No. The bully preys on the weak.

So what do we do? Well, someone is gonna have to man up, put their foot down, and kick him out of your house! When my mama kicked me out of the house, a long time ago, she said, "It's gonna hurt me from the bottom of my heart, but I'm gonna have to tell you to leave." Not ask me, but *tell* me to leave! We have to take that no-nonsense, enough is enough, "I had it up to here" attitude that my mom had with me.

Remember, David ran towards that giant "jabroni"

named Goliath, and threw a rock at him. We have to do the same. Some of my homeboys that have been in jail tell me that when you get locked up, you have to go up to the biggest, baddest inmate and just sucker-punch him in the jaw. That way you'll get your respect. (Now, I don't know if that's true, being that I've only been in prison to do ministry or to visit a cousin, but you'd have to give it some serious thought.) Davie-boy would not allow himself to be punk'd by a bully. Neither should we. Especially if our souls are at stake.

We need to do like Carrie Underwood and say, "Jesus, take the wheel!" Allow Jesus to regain control of your life. "Let go and let God." You see, David had a relationship with The Giant of giants. He knew that God had been with him when he went up against a lion and a bear. And he knew that God would help him defeat this Philistine Phenom, even if all he had was a rock. (It's no wonder the guy who wrote the Psalms describes God as a Rock[3] more than once.)

Earlier, I wrote that I would've given that woman at the red light the finger. Not the middle finger. (Take your mind out of the gutter! Ha!) I would've pointed my finger towards heaven reminding her that Jesus, who is God, is the Pilot and the Rock as well.

David trusted in God, and so does Carrie Underwood, according to her song. And you know who else? The apostle Paul did as well. Because even though he said that sin lived in him, he also said, so does God's Spirit.[4] If sin wants to make your life his home, so does God! So "move . . . get out the way!" have a seat, and grab some popcorn, cause the grits are about to hit the pan! It's on now! And we all know that God can kick the junk out of the devil, anywhere and anytime.

Anyway, isn't it easier to have the Landlord kick out that knucklehead tenant? Why waste your energy and stress yourself out? Let God do it. Give Him the number one spot in your life. And take counsel from a dude that's been through hell and back, our boy, Pablo: "Who will rescue me from this body of death? Thanks be to God—through Jesus Christ our Lord!"[5]

So who's flying your plane? You or Jesus?

---

1. See 1 Timothy 1:15, KJV.
2. Romans 7:15, 20.
3. Psalm 18:2, 31, 46.
4. 1 Corinthians 3:16.
5. Romans 7:24, 25.

CHAPTER FOUR

2 CATCH A THIEF

In the book, *At Jesus' Feet,* Doug Batchelor tells a story of a lost little kid. Maybe he was playing hide-and-go-seek, who knows? All we know is that he couldn't find his way back home. (Growing up extra large, I never had that problem. I could only hide behind big buildings.)

Anyway, Shorty sits down on a curb and starts crying. A police officer patrolling the streets sees the young buckaroo and asks him what is wrong. He tells the cop that he's lost and then asks for help. I imagine the cop mentioning street names in vain, while the little man becomes sadder and sadder.

It's like me. I'm no good at directions. (My wife, on the other hand, is the human MapQuest.) People give me directions like this: "Go the the Krispy Kreme and make a left. Then make a right at the Pizza Hut. Then go all the way down and pass the KFC . . ." (Anyways, enough about me. I'm getting hungry.)

So the police officer remembered the big church that's located in the center of town. From where they were, they could see the pinnacle of the church that had a humongous cross on top of it. He asks the little dude, "Do you live anywhere near that?"

"Yes!" the excited little kid says. "Take me to the cross. I can find my way home from there."

You know, "the cross still remains the starting place in the journey home for God's lost children."[1] Even the disciples, who walked with Jesus for three and a half years, really didn't start changing until they experienced the cross.

In this chapter I will focus on something awesome that happened on Redemption's Hill—at the cross. It's one of my favorite stories—the conversion of a convict, right smack in the middle of his death sentence. We don't even know his name. The Bible doesn't say much about the dude. We call him "the good thief," though. But he wasn't good! He was good for nothing! He wasn't even good at stealing. He got caught!

I believe this guy was a hard-core hooligan. Not like these wannabe gangstas from the suburbs that we see walking in the mall or even in some churches wearing Scarface shirts. This guy was pulling capers like Robert De Niro and Val Kilmer in that movie *Heat*. After all, I don't think they crucified people for just stealing lollipops. This guy was robbing federal banks, not bodegas. I also believe this dude was a murderer, like his homeboy Barabbas.[2]

The late Harry Williams broke down the introduction of this criminal kind of like this, in one of his sermons:

While Jesus was healing . . . this homeboy was stealing.

While Jesus was saying the beatitudes . . . this dude was
cursing out somebody's mama.

While Jesus was writing on the sand . . . homie was
tagging up the name of his gang in graffiti on the
walls of Jerusalem with spray paint.

And while Jesus resurrected somebody . . . this gangsta
was replenishing the graveyard by adding somebody
back in it!

Like another author said, this guy probably never said
grace, much less deserved it. But right there on death row,
when he was receiving capital punishment for his crimes, he
appealed for clemency.

Sometimes it takes a cross to catch a thief. And if God
saved him, there's hope for any one of us. Sometimes you got
to be down in order to look up.

Let's go back to the scene of the crime, and kind of dis-
sect it, *CSI: Miami*–style.

The Gospel of Matthew says that there were two crimi-
nals being crucified with Jesus; one on His left and the other
on His right. Above Jesus' head was a sign that read, "This is
the King of the Jews."

People were cracking and yelling all kinds of insults at
Jesus, even the two thieves. According to the Gospel of Luke,
one of the thieves (not the good one) says to Jesus, "Bro, ain't
you the man? Prove it. Save yourself, then hook us up too!"

This gets me a little mad. "Ain't you the man?" Of course,
He is! Even Pilate called Jesus the Man![3]

2 CATCH A THIEF

If I was Jesus, I would've interrupted the whole Crucifixion, just for a minute, to slap him from the cross. "Why you doubting?" *Whaaaaack!* Then, I would've told the Father, "You may proceed."

I imagine that that question must've hurt John's feelings when he heard it, being that he was the only disciple we know was at the crime scene. If I was him, I would've thrown my Timberland boots at him! Or I would've walked up to his cross and snapped his little pinky toe. "Say, 'Uncle!' "

This thief wanted something out of the deal. He didn't want a relationship with Jesus. He just wanted to get hooked up. Kind of like jailhouse religion. I know a lot of ex-cons that look for God while in prison, but when they come out, they go back to doing dirt. I think that's exactly what was happening on the cross.

He didn't really want to be saved by Jesus; he just wanted to be released. Maybe he wanted to go to the club that Friday night. Maybe he had a date with a Telemundo-looking mami. Or maybe he wanted to smoke one more blunt or drink one more forty. It's like when the multitude followed Jesus to see the miracles, or to scarf down the bread and the fishes.

I remember back in the hood, we had this big ol' rat terrorizing the whole block. I imagined this mouse beating Mickey up in school and stealing his lunch money. He was that big and bad. In fact, he looked like Splinter from the Ninja Turtles! At least, I think it was a rat—it could've been a mutt!

My sisters would complain to my parents because he was even chewing on their church shoes and making them open-toed.

I even had open-toe Adidas! (Though he never touched my brother's sneakers because that junk smelled like bad Fritos!)

One night my mama decided to set up a trap for this little joker, so we could finally get our peace back. She had my pops go to the Home Depot and buy the biggest mousetrap he could find—preferably the ones to kill alligators. That night they set up the trap, expecting to kill the rat before we got back from church. We didn't know whether to bait it with cheese or Kibbles 'n Bits.

Anyways, when we got home and turned on the lights, a million cockroaches fled. But we had bigger fish to fry. So we put our chanclas away. I checked out the trap and there he was, staring at me like "What?" His tail was pinned down to the trap, but his hips were moving like Shakira. I yelled for my brother to get the BB gun, while my mom and sisters flew on top of the couch.

Fifteen seconds later, I was face-to-face with the little rodent with gun in hand. I heard Michael Buffer in the background, saying, "Let's get ready to RUUUUUUMBLE!" I looked cautiously over my shoulders for Teenage Mutant Ninja Turtles. The coast was clear. I pointed the gun directly to his little head and said, in my best Arnold Schwarzenegger impersonation, "Hasta la vista, baby."

But the rat did the unimaginable. He ignored me! Me! The judge, jury, and executioner. I tried twirling my gun, pretending to be Jesse James, but nothing. He turned around with a little smirk and continued to eat off the cheese that was meant to be his last meal.

And that's exactly what happened at Calvary. The thief is caught in a little mousetrap of his own, but he continues to eat the cheese—instead of begging for mercy.

But the other thief—the good one, if you will—did. He said, "Yo, homie. You ain't scared? We deserve to die, cause we guilty, but Dude has done nothing wrong."

I like that about this good thief. He took responsibility for his own actions. I know a lot of people that do the opposite. Even Adam blamed God in Eden while Eve blamed the serpent. That's where we get that whole "the devil made me do it" thing.

I know people who leave church because when they were sick, nobody came and visited them. Or because the girls in their churches were stuck-up. Or because somebody talked junk about us. Come Judgment Day, we are gonna be judged individually. We're not going to be able to point the finger at no one but ourselves.

But not this dude. He had character. He declared himself guilty. He knew he was wrong. He wasn't trying to hide it. I see a lot of pastors at the pulpit trying to be holier than thou and me, wanting to be introduced with a mile-long résumé. They get on my nerve. I would love to shoot a spitball at them, at least once before I die. That's on my bucket list.

I think my ministry is effective because I admit to the congregation that I'm jacked-up, and am in desperate need of a Savior, still. I tell them that Jesus is the I AM, and I am NOT. Besides, the youth know if you're a phony. I tell them to pray for me as well. God knows I need it.

The good thief had no excuse. No public defender. Maybe his mama taught him that the truth would set him free. And indeed it did.

In the Old Testament of the Bible, something similar happened the night Jacob wrestled with an Angel. I imagine my man Jacob trying to Batista-bomb heaven's Messenger and putting Him in The Undertaker's triangle choke. Then the Angel, who was almighty and powerful, touched him on the hip with a finger and crippled him instantly. With a FINGER? Instantly. And made him limp for the rest of his life. That's old school hip-hop, right there! Even way before Run-D.M.C.! You know why? Because this wasn't any ordinary angel. He was going toe-to-toe with Jesus.[4]

"Let Me go," the Angel said.

But Jacob wouldn't do it. "No way," he said. "I'm not lettin' go until You bless me."

"What is your name?"[5] the Angel asked. Now why would Jesus, who is God, who knows even how many hairs we have on our head[6] (even the hair on some of y'alls ladies' weaves), ask him what his name was? Doesn't He know even the name of each of the stars?[7]

Check out what's happening. I think God, by asking him what his name was, was really asking him, as a Savior, to ask for forgiveness. And Jacob did. Just by saying his name, he admitted everything because the name *Jacob* means "cheater." "I am Jacob" could be translated to "I am a cheater, a liar, and a thief."

Then, Jesus said, "Now we talking, homie. That's what's

up! Today, you will be known as Izzy, or Israel!"

You see, God even changed his name so he wouldn't be reminded of his past! But he had to declare himself guilty first.

And that's what the good thief did. He pled "guilty as charged."

Back in the day, I used to work at Burger King. For those of you who have seen me, that explains a lot. My sister Lily was one of the managers there. One day I was hungry and tried to get hooked up with maybe a free hamburger, even though we could get them for half price. I asked her nicely if she could give me a Whopper with cheese. And my sister, who's always been by the book, said, "Nope!"

Not even a French fry! I was mad! You know what I did? That night I stole a box of one hundred Whoppers! I don't play!

I convinced my pops to be the getaway car, and everything! But I gave back to the community. I'm like Robin Hood. I gave hamburger meat to every family I knew. (So much for the health message!) I knocked on the door like I was the Godfather, and in my best Marlon Brando impersonation, I said, "I'll give you a Whopper you can't refuse."

I took the sixty that were left to my crib and grilled them with adobo. And no matter how good and how seasoned adobo makes our food taste, it still didn't compare to a Burger King Whopper. I was disappointed.

That night, while I was asleep, after the Babylonian feast I just had, my sister came home crying to my mother. "Mama,

I think they're gonna fire me. Somebody stole one hundred Whoppers, so they might write me up."

My moms, who had no clue (bless her heart), told her to calm down and get a glass of water. When my sister opened the refrigerator door, she yelled kind of like "Who's been eating my porridge?!"

Run, Goldilocks, run! "WIIIIIILLLLLLLLLLYYYYY!!" My named echoed throughout the projects! She woke me up by beating me with the high heels of her shoes! (In Spanish we call them tacos or tacones.)

Now imagine if she would've pressed charges on me. (Wait! Did somebody say "tacos"? *Mmm*.) What if my sister would've called the cops and ratted me out? Imagine me in jail, with a big brother named Tiny as a cell mate, talking about "What you in for?"

I couldn't tell him I was the Hamburglar! I'd have to tell him I shanked somebody or something! So, not only would I be a thief, I'd be a liar too. Sin only escalates.

And I couldn't have told the cops that I stole one hundred Whoppers because my sister didn't give me one!

I read somewhere that men do this all the time when they get mad at their wives. They turn to pornography. Or girls get mad with their boyfriends, so they wild out and end up on *Girls Gone Wild*. You see, that's our problem. We're always quick to blame someone else for our mistakes.

And this crucified crook could've done the same. But he didn't. He said, "I'm guilty." Then declares Jesus innocent.

Dude is transforming in front of all their eyes. He started

off dissing Jesus; now, he's protecting Him. I can imagine him whispering, "King of the Jews," as he reads the sign with a smile. Then he shocks everybody and cries out to Jesus and calls Him "Lord."

I remember once I was trying to put together a car model that I bought for my ex-girlfriend's son. It was hard. I couldn't get it. After messing with it for like an hour, I grabbed the instructions manual and took it to the bathroom. I took a glimpse at the little white book and just like that, I got it!

Same thing might've happened in the life of this career criminal. He tried to do it his way. He was hustling all his life. Stealing, cheating, and possibly even killing, to make it. It's the whole gangsta-rapper mentality. Until his sins finally caught up to him. Now he's hanging from a tree, in the middle of a Roman execution. He never got it right.

Until . . . until he took a look at the manual. Or, should I say . . . Emmanuel.

Then he rightfully called Christ, the Lord.

In doing that he was giving Jesus the props He deserves. In other words, he was calling Him King. Or Master. Ruler. (It's a shame these new versions of the Bible subtracted that part!)

And how about us? Do we do the same? Do we call Jesus "Lord" when we're at school, at work, or in the mall? How about at a restaurant? Do we even pray before we eat anymore?

I remember I was at a restaurant once, about to get my grub on with a few of my homies. We held hands and prayed for the food. When it was time to pay the bill, the waitress told us that we didn't have to pay a penny. Because somebody that saw us praying paid the bill for us! Can you believe that? Because we weren't embarrassed to call Jesus "Lord." When I thought about it, I got mad at the waitress. "Oh, now you tell me? I wanted to get two desserts! That flan was the bomb!"

Another time, I was preaching in Canada and the pastor took me to see Niagara Falls. I remember wondering to myself if the Flood might've caused such beauty. Then a busload of hippies lined up in front of me and bowed down before the mighty spectacle. I kind of smiled because I never seen something more ridiculous in my life, and I signaled over to the pastor to take a look.

Then this woman from the group catches me talking about them. (Well, I was really inquiring. But the way I went about it, laughing and pointing, I doubt will land me a part-time job as a journalist at *National Enquirer*!)

She walked up towards me like she was set tripping! She might've flashed a gang sign or two. I can't remember. But she comes up and asks me why I was laughing. Immediately, I apologized and asked her what they were doing. To my surprise, she said they were worshiping their god, Mother Nature.

When I smirked, she asked who my God was. What? She asked me about my God? Man, I got Robert De Niro on her. "YOU TALKING TO ME?"

It wasn't a time to be politically correct. I had to tell her. A lot of people don't want to hurt no one's feeling so they keep their mouth shut. Not me. Especially when it comes to this.

I told her my God is Jesus, the Creator of heaven and earth. "In fact, my God created your god!" Then I stuck out my tongue at her, and said, "Nani-nani-boo-boo!" Then I told the pastor, "Quick! Go start the car! Before we get lynched!"

This convicted felon, on the right hand of Jesus, did the same thing and he didn't care who heard him. A lot of people were ready to call Him "Lord" when He was performing miracles, but not one person acknowledged Him while He hung dying on the cross. Except for this ruffian. He called this crucified Carpenter "Lord." Because, sadly, it becomes a spiritual matter when you are just about dead. But better late than never, in his case.

Now if that didn't make you like the dude, check out what he did next. He tells Jesus to remember him when He comes back!

Yo, did you catch that? I still think some of yous didn't. He asks Jesus, in other words, "When You die, resurrect, go to heaven, and come back, holla at Your boy!"

Check out the faith on this brother! He became an Adventist on Calvary. Wow. How cool is that? Even Thomas and the disciples doubted the Resurrection, at first, even though He kept telling them He was going to die but rise again. Ellen White says, "Even some who profess to be looking for His appearing are no more prepared for that event than Satan himself."[8]

But homie told Jesus to remember him when He comes back. That's not a cry for his body, that's a cry for his soul.

A dead man is asking another dead Man to remember him? That's like me telling Fat Joe, "I'm a help you lose weight."

He finally understood that Jesus was the only way.

Wow. We can learn a lot from a thief and a gangster.

My boy, Roland, once taught me that lesson. Back in the days—before Christ—one of my other homies, who's a Marine, asked me to take care of his wife and kids while he was doing a tour in Japan. He just wanted me to check up on them from time to time. I did. But his wife began to catch feelings for me, or else she got real lonely. Because one day when I was on the phone with her she told me that she was taking a bath and wanted me to come over.

Then she messed up. She told me she wanted to have sex with me. You want to know what I did? I got on my knees and prayed.

Amen.

Psych! I got in the car so fast it looked like I was filming a remake of "The Fat & the Furious"! I looked like an over-stuffed Vin Diesel!

When I got to her door, I paused and decided to call my crime partner, Ro-Dawg, thinking that he would give me the consent to get busy. He didn't. He told me, "Willy, you should know better than that. Even though you ain't a Christian, I know your moms raised you better. Besides, that's your boy's girl. Get in the car and go back home and take a cold shower."

I was shocked (because Roland is more like Billy the Kid than Billy Graham), but I did what he said. Then he called me like twenty minutes later. "But Will, give me her number. I'll go see her!"

Today, I give thanks to God I didn't do either. But it took a thug to steer me back in the right direction. And hopefully, the story of this "good thief" does the same for you.

Check out Jesus' response. "I'm a tell you the truth today. You will be with Me in Paradise." Jesus told him, "Bro, before you die, I'm a make you a promise. When you wake up from the grave at My second coming, I'm taking you home with Me."

Somebody might disagree with me and say, "No. Jesus told him that TODAY he was going to be with Jesus!"

Well, I beg to differ. Sorry, that's not what He said. As the Greek was originally written, there was no punctuation. That refinement on literature did not develop until centuries after the writing of the Bible. Later translators had to decide where to put periods and commas. Since the popular teaching was that a person went directly to heaven or hell when they died, there was a strong political reason for translators to place the comma before the word *today* instead of after, completely changing the meaning of the verse.

A misplaced comma can communicate the total opposite meaning than what it was intended. For example, in the 1920s a wealthy stock trader sent his wife to Paris with some friends for her birthday. Before her return, she sent a Western Union telegram to her husband asking permission to purchase a stunning fox coat that cost $1,000. Her husband wired back his response: "No price too high." Thrilled by her husband's benevolence, she purchased the beautiful white coat.

When her husband met her at the ship, she disembarked wearing her lavish new rag. Her outraged spouse inquired, "Why did you buy the coat? I told you it was too expensive!"

Bewildered, she replied, "But, honey, you said no price was too high."

He shook his head. "I said, 'No, the price is too high!' " The telegraph office had neglected to put a comma after the word *no*.[9]

Regardless of where the comma goes, Jesus just pardoned this mafioso, and promised him eternal life. And if He did it for him, He'll do it for you.

I'll leave you with one more story that happened in New York fifteen to twenty years ago. One night two gangstas were so drunk and high, they decided to go rob somebody. The first person they encountered got beat-up and jacked. She was about sixty-two years old. She fainted. One of the thieves wanted more and decided to rape her. So he took her up to one of the rooftops of a building while the other thug was on the lookout.

When the elderly lady woke up and got a good look at the guy that was sexually molesting her, she screamed out, "Son! What are you doing?!"

The other thief recognized the woman's voice and told his friend, "Dude. You just raped your own mother." Devastated, he jumped off the building and killed himself.

The other one turned himself in, then later became a Christian and an evangelist.

There were two types of people on the New York rooftops that night. One chose death, the other chose life.

Same thing on Calvary. One chose death, and the other one was smart enough to choose life. I no longer wonder why the Bible didn't mention these two thieves' names. This way, we can see that this guy could have easily been me. It could have been my life. Or yours.

Unfortunately, there's two types of people right now, as well, reading this book. One will choose to die, to not accept Jesus Christ as Savior, while the other one will choose to do so and live forever.

Choose wisely.

In the old rugged cross,
stained with blood so divine,
a wondrous beauty I see,
for 'twas on that old cross Jesus suffered and died,
to pardon and sanctify me.

—George Bennard, 1873–1958

1. Doug Batchelor, *At Jesus' Feet: The Gospel According to Mary Magdalene,* 110.

2. Mark 15:7.

3. John 19:5.

4. Ellen G. White, *Patriarchs and Prophets,* 197.

5. Genesis 32:27.

6. Matthew 10:30.

7. Psalm 147:4.

8. Ellen G. White, *Testimonies for the Church,* 2:346, 347.

9. Doug Batchelor, *At Jesus' Feet,* 52.

CHAPTER FIVE

6 STEPZ 2 CHRIST

The whole church was in shock. No one could believe it. People started walking out. This lady had just screamed at the pastor and told him to shut up in the middle of his sermon.

A month after I got baptized, I was visiting a church with my boy, Eddie Gonzalez. The church was packed. We sat in the back. Somebody sang special music, then the pastor got up to preach. He was like twenty minutes into his sermon when the woman, who was sitting in front of us, got up from her chair and screamed out, "Shut up, Pastor!" I don't know if she was possessed or what, but I wasn't going to stick around to find out! I looked over at my homie and said, "Uh, I'll race you to the car, bro!"

I don't know about you guys, but I saw *The Exorcist* when I was like eleven, and I still get freaked out when I see a little white girl in pajamas! I was so scared I even held Eddie's hands! (Two grown men holding hands? If the church would've seen us, we probably would've got ex-communicated!) I didn't know what to do. And somehow I knew if I had said, "You betta stop playing!" she wouldn't have felt threatened at all.

The pastor kept preaching, but the more he kept going, the louder she got. She was going berserk. The stuff she was telling the pastor didn't make sense at all. At least to us it didn't. She even said something like, "Her blood is in your hand, Pastor!" Whatever that means. But it kind of sounded like she was bringing out some skeletons from his closet.

All of a sudden, this old-school deacon with a bow tie, who was sitting in the front, made his way down the aisle of the church and was face-to-face with the lady. I heard Superman's theme song in the background as he put his two hands on his hips. His tie even flapped like a superhero's cape.

He said, "I am Super Saved, defender of the law, and the church!" (Just kidding! That part didn't happen, but this part did . . .) He said, "In the name of Jesus of Nazareth, I rebuke you, Satan!" I came out from under the pew where I was hiding, expecting to witness a David and Goliath–type showdown. The church was silent, even the pastor stopped preaching. There I was in the middle of a real-life Mexican standoff. I even whistled that song in my head; you know, that one you hear in Clint Eastwood westerns.

Again old-school deacon said, "In the name of Jesus of Nazareth, I rebuke . . ." This time, he didn't get to finish the sentence. She interrupted him just like she had the pastor and said, "SIT DOWN, OLD MAN! NOW!" I thought to myself, *Maaan, if her head starts spinning around, I'm outta here!* (Run, fat Forrest! Run!)

I couldn't believe it. As I opened my eyes, I saw the deacon put his head down and start walking back to his seat.

What? This ain't how it's supposed to happen! David is supposed to kill Goliath. Elijah won on Mount Carmel. What's happening? Maybe he didn't fast and pray? (I sure didn't. The faster I eat, the better I feel!) Don't go, bro! At least hold her down while I hit her over the head with a steel chair! I watch TNA wrestling; I'll turn this into a six-sided ring, I don't care!

But he walked back to his seat. I looked over to Eddie and we were still holding hands. *Get off me, already!* I thought. I was upset. The cops had to come and remove her. Yep, the cops.

Now you don't have to be a student of the Holy Scriptures to know that there's power in the name of Jesus. In the name of Jesus, we can heal the sick. In the name of Jesus, dead men resurrect. And in the name of Jesus, we can definitely cast out demons, if that's what it was. So, what happened?

Maybe at night when nobody is looking, the defeated deacon crusader was a slave to sin. Satan probably laughed at him, and said, "You trying to give me orders?!" That brings me to the Bible quote I would like to share with y'all for this chapter. It's Joshua 3:5: "Joshua told the people, 'Consecrate yourselves, for tomorrow the LORD will do amazing things among you.'"

One of the meanings for the word *consecrate,* or *sanctify,* is to be free from sin. But how do we do that? The answer is Jesus Christ.

In Peter's first letter (1 Peter 4:8), he writes, "Love covers over a multitude of sins." And King Solomon takes it a step further, and says, "Love covers over ALL wrongs," in Proverbs 10:12 (emphasis added). So if we know that God is love, according to the Bible, what Pete and Solo are actually saying is this: "Jesus covers a multitude of sins, in fact, He covers all wrong."

Pastor Alvin Payne once said in a sermon, "The more you love Jesus, the more your sins are covered, because you ain't gonna want to sin." Here's a six-step program that I try to use to get closer to God. Check it out. See if it works for you.

1. We need to have a RELATIONSHIP with God.

This is a must! Pastor Sergio Torres, or as I call him, Master Yoda, once described it as a "love affair." A lot of people know of Jesus, but don't know Him personally. They know the twenty-eight doctrines of the church, but don't have a single clue about *who* they point to. They're lost inside the church, just like the parable of the lost coin.[1] That's why we need to be cemented in Him.

I remember one of my friends, Eddie, who is a United States Marine, telling me he had to leave his family when his youngest son Gaby was just two years old. He was stationed at Guantanamo Bay for two years but would call his family in Virginia almost every day. So in a way, he had a long-distance relationship with his infant son.

Gaby was getting to know his father over the phone. When it finally came time for Ed to come home, his family smothered him with hugs and kisses. All except Gaby. He hid behind his mother at the sight of this stranger and started crying. But when he heard his father's voice, he would smile. The father would have to win the little kid's confidence by talking. Gaby didn't know the face, because he hadn't seen it. But he knew the voice.

And ditto with us. We need to start having an awesome relationship like that with God, the kind of relationship where even though we don't see His face, we still know His voice when He speaks.

We need to invite Jesus to go everywhere we go and to be in every conversation we have. Invite Him to the mall with you when you're buying clothes. Take Him to work with you. I once worked at a place where I used to have to punch in at 6 A.M. But my boss didn't get there until 7 A.M. So from 6 to 7, me and my homeboy would sit around talking, eating donuts, and drinking hot chocolate.

I wasn't working. What I was doing was stealing from my employer. Keep in mind, I wasn't a born-again Christian at the time. But still, sometimes I go places and I leave God in the car. Some of us leave Him in the church—and just visit Him on the weekend. How do we expect to make it without Christ? That's like jumping off a plane without a parachute! The Christian life is a "mission impossible" without Jesus. We need to invite Him everywhere we go, except maybe the bathroom! He can probably wait outside for that one.

But even in our conversations, He's absent. I know a lot of professed Christians that curse more than Tony Montana! Gangstas apologize to me when an *F* word slips their mouth, yet some church folk just don't care.

One of my friends is *GQ* smooth. Good-looking dude. He was a "playa-playa" back in the day. Then he got married. One day I went to the mall with him and he was flirting with a girl that was not his wife! He took off his ring and everything. He even got the girl's number. When I asked him what he was doing, he told me not to worry because he wasn't gonna call her. He just wanted to know if he "still had it."

One time, he almost got busted. He was with his wife, and he ran into the girl that he met at the mall. Dude was red! He looked like Bob the Tomato. Luckily for him, she never said anything. My man likes to flirt around with disaster. And so do we all. We flirt around with the devil every chance we get. Even when we rent movies. We tell Satan, "Let's make it a Blockbuster night!" Why not invite Jesus instead? After all, isn't He with us always[2] anyways?

When Lynette, Christian, and I go visit my parents in Hollywood, Florida, we try to make it a fun road trip for three hours. That can be tricky, especially with a six-year-old kid. We talk, laugh, and carry on a lot. But there comes a time in our trip where we are completely silent.

We stop talking to each other. Christian is daydreaming. Wifey is humming a song. And I'm playing my PSP. (We're driving her car. Mine don't have AC!) But still, we are aware of each other's presence. The same thing has to be done in our Christian walk. Always be aware of His presence and start loving Him with all our heart, with all our soul, with all our mind, and with all our strength.[3]

How would you describe your relationship with Jesus?

2. We need to READ the Bible more.

How are we gonna have a relationship with someone, when we don't know them? The Bible helps us get to know Him.

And not only that, "It transforms the nature and re-creates the soul."[4] The apostle Paul's advice to Timothy in his letter was to devote himself to the reading of Scripture.[5] Maybe that's how, as somebody once said, readers become leaders.

I read the front page of a young person's Bible once and somebody dedicated it to them in this manner: "Sin keeps you from this Book, but this Book keeps you from sinning."

I ain't trying to show off or nothing, but I love reading. I hardly watch TV because of it. It's one of my hobbies. I read on the plane, before I go to sleep, and sometimes, I hook up a bubble bath and read a good Max Lucado or Ellen White book. But you know what? The Bible is the only Book that reads me. The pastor that baptized me, Idalberto Torres, once said in a sermon, "Your salvation depends on the dedication you give to the Bible, because the Bible points you to Jesus, who is salvation."[6]

The Bible is our soul food. It has it all; sex, hope, violence, love, everything. But what it really is, is a love letter written in red ink, the blood of a Jewish Carpenter.

Ladies are awesome when it comes to writing love letters. Some men are too. (Like yours truly. I'm old school. Sometimes I still take time out to write one for Gatita. I write poems, and everything. I once wrote a girl, "My life without you is empty . . . like church service on Wednesday nights!") Ladies spray on perfume and leave red lipstick prints. We guys, though we don't like to admit it, go nuts for that kind of stuff. But now, with e-mails and text messaging, we don't take the time out to write a long love letter anymore. And a lot of us don't take the time to read the Bible anymore, either.

Every time I'm on my way home from preaching, the enemy whispers in my ear, *Take a break from reading today. You did good.* He tries to make me believe that I don't need to study the Word! And you know what? Sometimes I believe him. I feel like I deserve time off. That's very dangerous.

I remember when I was little—well, uh, I never was "little"—OK, I remember when I was younger (that might be better), I used to write love letters to the girlies in middle school. The question I always ended with was, "Do you love me? Check Yes or No."

Today, God is asking you the same.

3. We need to PRAY more.

There's power in prayer! My moms prayed for ten years that I'd give my life to Christ! I heard somebody say once that "prayer will move the Arm that moves the world." And Satan knows that. In fact, he and his crew tremble at the sound of fervent prayer.[7] Prayer is communicating with God. That's why the enemy hates it. He doesn't want you to reach out to the Savior. If he had his way, we'd all be dead. That's why he tries to discourage us. Satan ain't a player-hater, he's a prayer-hater!! I tease him sometimes and pretend I'm getting on my knees! "Don't make me pray, booooy!"

I remember I used to love watching horror movies. It's basically all the same. A fly little white girl running away from a serial killer. She could be getting chased by Michael Myers, Jason, or Freddy. It doesn't matter. She always ends up running to hide inside a parked car. And the car can be brand-spanking new, but it never starts! So the girl runs into a house to call the police. And guess what? The phone doesn't work, either! Not because they didn't pay the bill, though that might be the case if she was in the hood, but because the killer cut the cord.

Well, that's exactly what Satan tries to do. Cut our cord. He tries to disconnect our phone line so we won't call God for help. Don't let him. When the enemy tries to cut your landline, you break out your celly! Yeah, how come them girls in the movies don't have cell phones? How in the world is that possible in this day and age when everybody and their mama has one? Daniel prayed three times a day.[8] But that was the Old Testament. In the New Testament, Paul said "pray all the time."[9]

After all, we take a bath daily, don't we? (Well, most of us do. I can smell somebody's stank armpits from here. Why you blushing?) Ellen White says that "no man is safe for a day or an hour without prayer."[10]

Pray. Talk to God as if you were talking to a friend. Don't just tell Him what you think He wants to hear. Your prayers will get stale or boring. Martin Luther was quoted as saying, "Woe to me, for even my prayers have become lukewarm." That's exactly why you need to tell God everything. Make it juicy. If you're gonna gossip about somebody, gossip to Him. Tell Him first before you tell a friend. Do you run to the throne or run to the phone? (Share your desires with Him. And your likes, your dislikes, your dreams, and your pain.) He can be like your diary.

I see a lot of people on Facebook updating their status every hour. (That's one of my pet peeves, to be honest.) They let the world know everything that they're doing. Twitter is way worse! People text about what they're gonna eat, what they're gonna do, what they're gonna watch. (I wish somebody would dare to write when they're going to the bathroom! That'll be funny.) But if only we would treat God like a Facebook update. Then we would be better off. It is a privilege to talk to God. "What other nation is so great as to have their gods near them the way the LORD our God is near us whenever we pray to him?"[11]

One time, my mother asked me to pray for my little niece, Gigi. She had a case of double pneumonia and it looked like she was gonna die. I wasn't even baptized yet, but I prayed for her nonetheless. I kind of bargained with God. I said, "God, I done lived my life. I met Al Pacino, J.Lo, Hulk Hogan. I had my Cadillacs and my share of girlfriends. So let's do this: Take my life but let her live. She's young and has her whole life ahead of her. What do You say? Deal or no deal?" The next morning, Gigi was jumping around on the playground outside! Everybody was jumping for joy. Yeah, everybody, except me. I ran for cover, in case God decided to strike me with a bolt of lightning! I was like, "I was just kidding, God! Psych! Look, I had my fingers crossed."

But a deal is a deal. God did take my life that day. In the streets I was known as the Latin Assassin, now I'm Willy Ramos, ghetto preacher! So go ahead, dial God's number. Anytime. Anywhere. This young lady once told Pastor Alejandro Bullón that when she prayed, she felt that the prayer never even made it past the ceiling. He told her to try praying outside, then.

One day, before I was married, I was at the flea market and this hot-looking Spanish mamasita was checking me out big time! She must've thought I was Big Pun or Fat Joe, cause she couldn't keep her eyes off me. I was working up my nerves to try and talk to her when she walked up towards me! She told me something like this: "You are hotter than Brad Pitt, George Clooney, Johnny Depp, and Denzel, combined!" (OK, maybe I'm exaggerating, but, for reals, it was something to that effect!)

Then she asked me to go over to her house that night. "Wait a minute," I said, kind of scared, "chill out! Take it easy lady. I don't even know your name!" She looked at me stunned, like she was gonna hit me over the head with her purse! She said, "What are you talking about?" I said, "You just invited me to your house!" Turns out, she wasn't even talking to me. She had on a Bluetooth. You should've seen me, I was red! And fat. Somebody shouted, "Hey, Kool-Aid!"

One more analogy. I have this homeboy by the name of Rico. I called his cell phone one day, but we had bad reception. I was trying to talk to him like three whole minutes! I did the whole Verizon thingy and everything! "Can you hear me now? Can you hear me now?" It was like he couldn't hear me, but I could hear him. Then I hear him say, "Ha! I got you. This is a recording. Leave your message after the beep." What, a "recording"? I hate when people get me. It makes me wanna punch somebody in the face! Wait 'til I see him! I'm a throw this cell phone right upside his big head! Watch!

So why the "me getting dissed" analogies? Because with God, there is no miscommunication. When you pray, you are talking directly to the Source. He does not have a secretary. He picks up the phone Himself. Why not try calling Him today? Or at least send Him a "knee mail."

4. Run from temptation.

Don't roll with the punches, dodge from them! Just like Joseph, you need to haul butt when you see temptation coming!

I have this homie, who every time he calls me, he asks to borrow money. Now I don't mind lending, if I have some, but this brother don't pay up! (If you're reading this, pay up, fool!) So now what I do is check the caller ID when my phone rings. If it says his name, I press "Ignore."

That's the same thing we have to do with temptation. When a fine woman passes by, when you hear a song on the radio, when you turn on the TV, check the caller ID. If it says, "Satan," then you hit "Ignore." The Bible says, "Resist the devil, and he will flee."[12] "Jesus does not desire those who have been purchased at such a cost to become the sport of the enemy's temptation. He does not desire us to be overcome and perish. He who curbed the lions in their den and walked with His faithful witnesses amid the fiery flames is just as ready to work in our behalf."[13]

So our prayer should be like the one found in Matthew 6:13, "Lead us not into temptation, but deliver us from the evil one."

I used to look at the girls in church with their miniskirts

on and I'd be like, "Lord, have mercy! *¡Reprende a Satanás!*
¡Reprende a Satanás! ¡Reprende a Satanás!" I heard a quote one
day from the pulpit that impacted me, so I had to write it in
my Bible. It says,

Watch your thoughts, for they become words.
Watch your words, for they become actions.
Watch your actions, for they become habits.
Watch your habits, for they become character.
Watch your character, for it becomes your destiny.

It's sad to say, but, sometimes, we tempt the devil to
tempt us.

That's like me going into an "all you can eat" restaurant
when I'm on a diet! ("I'll just have a salad." Yeah right! The
only time I eat lettuce and tomato is on a Whopper!) It's like
the dude that walked up to Satan, and said, "How dare you
tempt me? I belong to God!" Satan answered, "If you belong
to God, what are you doing in my territory?" Martin Luther
said, "You can't help if the birds fly around your head, but
you can prevent them from making a nest there." How do
you handle temptation?

5. Keep your eyes fixed on Jesus!

Pastor José Antonio Pagan from the Jesus Loves Jeans ministry puts it this way, "The minute you stop looking at Jesus, there's
an alarm that goes off in Satan's office. Then he sends out an 'all
points bulletin' and tells the pit bulls of hell to go and 'sic' you!"

"Our only hope is in 'looking unto Jesus the Author and Finisher of our faith.' "[14] We even have a hymn about it. Don't look at the pastor. Don't look at the elders. In fact, don't look at me, either! Cause, man, I might steer you to hell by mistake! Look to JESUS!

When Peter had his eyes fixed on Jesus, he moonwalked on top of water. But when he started paying attention to his surroundings, he sank and almost drowned! Dr. Tony Evans said, "What began as a step of faith, ended up as a belly flop!"

I once I dated a girl from Trinidad who had a four-year-old son. One day he got the flu, and woke up with a lot of green, gross-looking stuff they called "yampi" (That name sounds so gross, I almost threw up typing this!) coming from his eyes. He couldn't even see. He bumped into the wall twice. A lot of us need to clean the "yampi" from our eyes and look to God. Or else pretty soon, we gonna bump our heads as well.

We have a song in the Hispanic churches called "Dame La Mano." I guess it's translated as "Gimme Your Hand." It's whack. I don't like it much. But we swear by it. It's our Pledge of Allegiance. Here's why I don't care too much for it. It says, "If your heart is just like mine, gimme your hand, and my brother you'll be." If your heart is just like mine? Who are we kidding? If your heart is like mine, you're more lost than the cast of that ABC TV show!

Bro, my "heart is hopelessly dark and deceitful."[16] Out of it comes "evil thoughts, murder, adultery, sexual immorality, theft"[17] and lies! Don't follow me, follow Jesus! He's the Man!

6. Throw away that rotten sandwich!

When one of my best friends, Casper, was down on leave from the military, he invited me to go eat at an Italian restaurant. And being that I love me some pasta and pizza, I agreed. (My wife and I love Olive Garden! I'm there so much, one day somebody confused me with the manager!) I told him I was goin' to meet him after I ran some errands for my moms first. So we agreed to meet later.

Well, later came and I forgot about my friend. I went to the neighborhood bodega called Busy Bee in North Lauderdale that has the best submarine sandwiches (I call them manna from heaven) in the world, and bought me a footlong! That sub was so big, it had actual sailors jumping out of it as I inhaled the first few bites. I looked like Pac-Man—you should've seen me!

Then my homeboy called. "Oops! My bad. I'll be right there." And even though I was meeting him for dinner, I ate half of the sub. I kept it on the DL, so my homie wouldn't think I was greedy. (I forgot that back in the day, he witnessed me drive up to a complete stranger on the streets who was eating Doritos and snatch his bag. Then I took off faster than Speed Racer!)

Even though the sandwich was the bomb, I threw the other half away. What? What are you, crazy? I did what any fat person would've done; I saved it for a late-night snack to eat it when I'm watching *George Lopez* or *Jay Leno*! But I didn't have time to go drop it off at home, so I put it inside the glove compartment of my car. Not wise at all. It was like ninety-five degrees that day and I had extra onions on my sub.

By the time I picked up Casper, my car was smelling like feet and armpits! He got in and right away wanted to throw up. He looked at me with disgust and screamed, "Eww, homie! Sorry to say this, but did you take a bath? You stink so bad you made Right Guard turn left!"

I opened up the glove compartment and exposed the rotten sandwich. I wasn't about to be labeled Pepé Le Pew. I already had fat jokes to fight off. Homie looked at me like if he felt sorry, with a "we need to do an intervention soon" look, and said, "Man, you're fat!"

A lot of us, or maybe I should say most of us, have rotten sandwiches inside the glove compartment of our lives. A cherished sin. We love it. When nobody is looking, we're on cloud nine, whether it be on our computers at night when everyone is sleeping or alone watching TV. But pretty soon, that sin is gonna start stinking. "One sin cherished is sufficient to work the degradation of the character."[18]

Judas, Balaam, and the rich young ruler, let their love for money bring them down. Is there a sin in your life that's threatening to bring you down, as well? Is there a skeleton in your closet?

That submarine sandwich left me so full that I really didn't eat much at the Italian restaurant—and that one bite of sin can leave you so full that you won't want to eat at the wedding supper of the Lamb.

"If you give yourself to Him, and accept Him as your

Saviour, then, sinful as your life may have been, for His sake you are accounted righteous. Christ's character stands in place of your character, and you are accepted before God just as if you had not sinned."[19]

"Consecrate yourselves, for tomorrow the LORD will do amazing things among you."[20]

---

1. Luke 15:8–10.
2. Matthew 28:20.
3. Mark 12:30.
4. Ellen G. White, *Education,* 126.
5. 1 Timothy 4:13.
6. See Luke 19:9.
7. Ellen G. White, *Testimonies for the Church,* 1:346.
8. Daniel 6:10.
9. 1 Thessalonians 5:16–18, *The Message.*
10. Ellen G. White, *The Great Controversy,* 530.
11. Deuteronomy 4:7.
12. James 4:7.
13. Ellen G. White, *My Life Today,* 317.
14. Ellen G. White, *Testimonies for the Church,* 5:199, 200.
15. Matthew 14:29.
16. Jeremiah 17:9, 10, *The Message.*
17. Matthew 15:19.
18. Ellen G. White, *The Desire of Ages,* 439.
19. Ellen G. White, *Steps to Christ,* 62.
20. Joshua 3:5.

CHAPTER SIX

IN DESPERATE NEED OF A SAVIOR

A homeless man walked up to me and one of my homeboys, years ago, and asked us a question. "Are you guys down with the Nation?" We thought he was asking us if we were in favor of the Nation of Islam, so right away we said, "No." "Unless you have some bean pies, because I am mighty hungry," I added jokingly. "We Christians."

Homeless dude looked at me confused. "What? Bean pies? Christians? What are you talking about? I didn't ask you if you were down with the 'Nation,' I asked if you are down with do-na-tion! Got a dollar?" Ha. That line was so original, we each gave him two dollars. He made out like a bandit.

In this chapter, I wanna talk about another beggar. But we find his story in the Bible. This man had two problems. He was begging people for money, so he might've been homeless as well, and he needed a doctor. Not like Dr. Dolittle, Dr. Phil, Dr. Dre, or Dr Pepper. This guy needed an optometrist, cause he was blind.

Two thousand years ago, there was not one doctor

performing laser eye surgery, so he needed a special kind of doctor. He needed a Divine Medic, a Specialist of Miracles. He needed Dr. Jesus of Nazareth. In fact, we all need Him to heal us from sin. We are all sinners, not only because we break the law (it's not only the action we do), but it's the condition we were born in. The worse you are, the more you need Jesus.

Lemme tell you this blind man's (Bartimaeus) story from Luke 18:35–42. Check out this dude's desperate attempt to get Jesus' attention.

Jesus, His boys, and a crowd of other people were almost to Jericho.[1] "Bart" heard all the ruckus and asked what was going on. He must've felt like he was in the Calle Ocho festival in Miami! Jesus (Dr. J) is passing through, someone told him.

Imagine the goose pimples the brother got when he heard that. Dude probably got butterflies in his stomach. (I had a celebrity crush on Jennifer Lopez, back in the day, and every time I heard her name I felt butterflies, birds, bats, and midgets wrestling inside mine! Or maybe I was just hungry . . . who knows.)

Here was the Answer to his problem. The Miracle Maker was just a few feet away from him. So dude started yelling loud, like if he was a Puerto Rican. We are LOUD. (One Sabbath I was preaching in church and the people in the sound booth had my mic up a little too much. So I signaled them to turn it down just a bit. They never did. When I finished, I went to the back and asked why they didn't turn it down. They said, "Bro, your microphone was never on. We forgot to put batteries in it.")

Anyways, Bart screamed out, "Dr. J! Hook me up, pleeeeease!" He let his soul cry out! He probably did an ugly face too. I don't know if you've noticed, but the best singers in the world make the ugliest faces when they hit the high notes. Yuck! It doesn't matter how fine they are, or if it's Mariah, Celine, or Whitney. Every time they hit a high note, they make the ugliest face, like they're turning into a werewolf or something.

Well, that's how I pictured Bart. Screaming like his life depended on it! "Paging Dr. Jesus! Paging Dr. Jesus!" Do you remember the last time you paged Him? Have you ever cried out to Jesus like that?

Now I don't know who told my man, Bart, that Jesus was a Healer but by the way he was screaming out, he knew! Maybe his mother taught him about Jesus when he was a shorty. Maybe he heard that Jesus healed another blind man just by putting mud and saliva on the dude's eyes.[2] (I would've just said, "Nah, Jesus, just say the word and I'll be healed!" Saliva?!)

But check out what happens to Bartimaeus. Sometimes, I read the Bible and something in it makes me so mad. Like when the Bible tells me to love my enemies[3] (I don't wanna love them, I wanna beat them up!), or when it says not to eat pork[4] (Man, I used to love me some chuletas!). But enough about who I wanna beat up and what I wanna eat, look what makes me mad about this story.

The peeps that were walking with Jesus told him off, and told the dude to shut up! "Those who led the way rebuked him and told him to be quiet."[5] What? Those who led the way? The church? Church folk get on my nerves sometimes. Tyler Perry as Madea once said, "Church is fine . . . my problem is church folk."[6] And it's true! Sometimes we think we're holier than everybody and their mamas! Especially us Adventists! Just because we keep the Sabbath day holy like the Bible commands, we think we are the only ones that are gonna make it to heaven. But no.

Did you know that there's gonna be a lot of Baptists in the New Jerusalem? And a lot of Pentecostals and Lutherans? Even a lot of Jews will believe in Christ and help us spread the word about God's return before the end![7] And, yes, Catholics also. And if we are lucky, there's gonna be a lot of Seventh-day Adventists there as well.

We mistake the Sabbath for the truth. The Sabbath is NOT the truth! I repeat: the Sabbath is NOT the truth. Jesus said, "I am the way and the truth and the life."[8] You see, Jesus is the Truth. And, because I love Him who is the Truth, I will obey Him when He tells me to keep the Sabbath Day holy.[9] Our religion won't save us, but our relationship with Him will.

I had the privilege on more than one occasion to preach at some Catholic churches. The priests knew what my religion was, but invited me nonetheless. Because this is life or death. We don't wanna lose our youth and they don't either. So they tell me to preach about Christ and Him crucified. And you know what? I do.

IN DESPERATE NEED OF A SAVIOR

Don't get me wrong; I ain't a dumb brotha either. I take advantage sometimes and let them know that on Saturday when I was in church, I was blessed by my pastor's sermon. Then after the service, they usually ask me where I go to church and I witness to them. One time when I was done preaching, even the nuns came and gave me high fives! I felt like Whoopi Goldberg in *Sister Act*. Imagine me in a remake called *Brotha Act*!

We get cocky. We want everyone to look like us and dress like us. Maybe that's exactly why those that were leading the way, walking with Jesus, rebuked poor Bartimaeus. Maybe he still smoked cigarettes or still went to Starbucks for his caffeine fix. Maybe Bart would let his pants sag so much you could see his underwear like some street brothers do. He probably didn't wear ties for church on Sabbath. (I buy my ties at the flea market, three for ten dollars. A three-dollar tie does not turn me into SuperSalvo and make me holier than thou!) Or maybe he was a drummer in a band or wore a wedding ring or ate KFC. (I know a lot of people that don't eat meat, but overdose on gluten!) A lot of us worship the temple and not the God of the temple!

Years ago, my brother Papo, who as of yet has not received Christ as Savior, decided to go to church with us. My parents and I are the only ones baptized, so we were extremely happy. "This could be the day that God touches him," my mother said excitedly. I prayed that He would.

When we got to church, I told them that I had to go to the bathroom, so my brother and my parents walked inside without me. But I didn't have to use the bathroom. I was calling one of my mentors, Richard Guerrero, who has prayed for my family since I've known him, to tell him the good news that my brother is inside the church. When I finished, my moms told me that somebody just rebuked my brother for having long hair! Long hair?! They told him that only women have long hair and he should cut it off. My brother was visiting the church and this is how we treated him. Pastor Bill Crofton once said about a similar case, "The last time the Bible records someone having to cut his hair, it cost Samson his eyes!"

You know what the problem is? We don't have deacons in our churches anymore, we have bouncers! We have airport security! I have been preaching for ten years of my life, bringing kids back to the foot of the cross, and somebody kicked my brother out. It ain't fair.

You know, 'til this day, I don't know who did it. And I wanted to know. I was mad! I wanted to backslide just for two minutes to knock somebody out. I wanted to give somebody a knuckle sandwich. The Bible does say it's better "to give than to receive"![10]

Today, my brother is still in the world because those that "led the way rebuked him." I tell him not to take it out on God. God didn't kick him out, Satan did. But I would understand if he never came back. We turn people off sometimes.

When I got baptized, an elder told me that I wasn't gonna last one year in the church! Another person (a youth leader) told me that his youth program was gonna be ten times better than mine. I got mad, but I shouldn't of. If God uses somebody ten times better than me, well, hallelujah!

I remember hearing a story about a guy that was angry at the devil for breaking up his marriage. He wanted to fight him, so he went to look for him. He went into a strip joint to see if he could find him, but he didn't. He went into a bar and into a club, and still the devil was nowhere to be found. Until he walked into a church. The devil walked up to him and said, "I heard you were looking for me."

Please don't get me wrong, I do love my church. I heard Pastor J "Figz" once say that "church is our rescue boat." And it is. I'm pretty sure Noah's ark smelled like animal doo-doo, but it was necessary for them to be there in all that stench in order to be saved.

No matter how jacked up our church is, it's necessary for us to be there. "Let us NOT give up meeting together, as some are in the habit of doing, but let us encourage one another—and all the more as you see the Day approaching."[11]

But we need to "encourage" each other, not tear each other down just because a woman wears pants to church! How old school is that?!

But let us not read the Bible too fast. Verse 39 ends well. Even though the church was trying to rebuke my man Bart, he shouted even louder. If at first he was louder than a Boricua at the Puerto Rican Day Parade, now he's making people's ears bleed with a megaphone! I like this blind man's determination.

All my life I heard, "If at first you don't succeed, try and try again." My homie, an ex-gangsta named Krusho, once told me, "If at first you don't succeed, cheat, I say." (I caught him slipping one night with a bunch of "Draw Four" Uno cards under his baseball cap!)

I remember I was rebuked from a pulpit once because of my sunglasses. And they were prescriptions! And even though it was discouraging, I'm still here. Amen? Another dude didn't wanna go do mission work with me because he said I look like a gangsta. He had some nerve!

He looked nerdier than Steve Urkel, but I didn't care! You know what I did? I took off my glasses and put on a tie! Because I am not gonna let nothing or nobody stop me from doing what God has called me to do! Besides, Pastor Manny Cruz, another one of my mentors, once told me, "Never wrestle a pig. Because you both get dirty, and the pig likes it."

Now, let's ignore what Krusho said and did and learn from the Bible and what Bart did. He kept praying even though God didn't answer him right away. I can picture him telling the people that told him to be quiet, "You shut up! Besides, I ain't talking to you!"

Before I was baptized, my brother and I went to the movies a lot. And we don't know how to act sometimes. Once, my brother, who was real fat, broke the chair. As I pointed and laughed at him, my chair broke as well. I was fatter. But my brother must've broke the whole system. The preppy older people would tell us, "*Shhh.* We're trying to watch a movie."

Immediately, my brother would respond with a "No. You *shhh*." He wasn't gonna let anyone tell him what to do. Bartimeaus wasn't gonna let no one either. Especially when it came to his eyesight. What Jesus says and does is what matters.

Have the doctors told you that you only have a few months to live, because that cancer is going to kill you? Has somebody ever told you you're never gonna make it in life? Has Satan lied to you and made you believe that you'll never break that addiction?

It doesn't matter what people say—it matters what Jesus says. A lot of people worry about how people look at them and say things about them. Not Bart. He said, "Later for y'all, I need HELP! I need a miracle! I need a Savior!" That's when Jesus, the Creator of heaven and earth, stopped to hear him out. Wow.

Then He ordered them to bring Bart over. He didn't say, "Tell him to come here." He said, "Bring him to Me." The same people that were dissing him were now told to bring him to Jesus by the Master Himself. "For whoever exalts himself will be humbled."[12]

Jesus looked at him and said, "What you need, homie?" And he answered, "I just wanna see." And God hooked him up. Right then and there! Though the church dissed him, he got to see the color of God's eyeballs. Ironic. Of all the people on the road that day, Bartimeaus was the one "with the clearest vision"[13] even before the miracle.

I can imagine the following Sabbath a youth director asking

him if he can sing special music for divine worship. He agrees to. He sings "Amazing Grace," by John Newton. The church gives him a standing ovation and they praise God for what He did. Not when the song is over, but around the part when he says, "I once was blind, but now I see." What is your need? What would you like God to do for you?

"A person that refuses to see is worse than someone that is blind" (a Spanish proverb).

1. Mark 10:46.
2. John 9:1–6.
3. Matthew 5:44.
4. Leviticus 11:7, 8.
5. Luke 18:39.
6. Tyler Perry, *Don't Make a Black Woman Take Off Her Earrings: Madea's Uninhibited Commentaries on Love and Life*, 210.
7. Ellen G. White, *Manuscript Releases*, 1:137.
8. John 14:6.
9. Exodus 20:8–11.
10. Acts 20:35.
11. Hebrews 10:25; emphasis added.
12. Matthew 23:12.
13. Max Lucado, *And the Angels Were Silent*, 38.

CHAPTER SEVEN

BIG POCKETS OR BIG HEAD?

I remember reading a book awhile back by Max Lucado—or was it Mark Finley? Though I can't remember the author, the story still haunts me, for it was based on a true one. About a life or death choice we all have to face, sooner or later.

The book was about a millionaire youth pastor who was a Seventh-day Adventist. Rumor had it he had so much money Oprah asked him for a loan! This guy had it all. He was an awesome speaker. Guys admired him and single girls got butterflies every time he grabbed the mic. Even the married ladies elbowed their husbands when he preached and asked, "Why can't you be like him?" I imagine the brother looking like Tyrese with a six-pack, and everything. (People like that get on my nerves. I have six two-liters! Or a keg. College kids like to hang around me.)

He had designer clothes and name-brand watches. Dude had a big mansion, one that MTV would've been proud to film an episode of *Cribs* in. And his ride? Whaat? It was already pimped—Xhibit didn't have to do nothing. A Lexus—2013!

One day after church, he was driving his car down the boulevard listening to the latest by Casting Crowns. He stopped at a red light and noticed something fishy. To the right of him was a park and it look like a kid's birthday party was taking place. Cake, Doritos, pizza, a bounce house, and a . . . man blessing the kids and praying for them, kind of like the pope does.

"There's something rotten in Denmark," he said to himself as he put his tinted window down just by touching his steering wheel. (I still have to roll mines down with my hand! Sometimes the little lever thingy comes off, and I have to put it back on!) He, being curious, parked the car on the side of the road and headed for the party. I can imagine him walking in slow motion and his trench coat flapping in the wind, like John Travolta's in *Face/Off.*

All of a sudden, the guy in question spots him and starts walking away. "Rockefeller" wasn't about to let him go that easy, so he started running towards him. Then he did something that must've stunned everybody who witnessed it, from the mothers to the bebe kids. He got on his knees!

Oh, I remember the author now . . . his name was Mark.

Mark, last name: Ten.

Middle name: Chapter.

Mark chapter 10. Let's read verse 17 thru 22: "As Jesus was about to take off, this dude who was loaded with crazy dough runs up to Him and falls on his knees. He gives Him props by calling Him, 'Good Teacher,' then asks, 'What I gotta do to get hooked up with eternal life?' " (my own paraphrase).

Before I continue, let me point out three things that homie did that I like. We preachers take this story of the rich young ruler and tell congregations not to be like him. But what we fail to tell you is that he started off right.

First of all, dude came to Christ with the right attitude. He gave Jesus much props when he bowed down to Him. (That's like Donald Trump or P. Diddy, in an Armani suit, kneeling down in front of a riffraff. Imagine that!)

We don't even pay Him that much respect! We leave our baseball caps on when we're praying, we talk while the pastor is preaching, and we constantly come late to church. I saw a member come to church in a wifebeater and flip-flops! Now don't get me wrong. I'm all for this "Come As You Are" movement; in fact, every Wednesday night, my family and I attend C.A.Y.A. in Forest City Spanish Church. (Tania, you're doing an awesome job, may God expand your territory.) But if you're coming to church for like three years and you still haven't changed, then you better check yourself. Of course, "God loves you just the way you are, but He refuses to leave you that way."[1]

The second thing I like about dude is that he came to Jesus as a young buck. I know a lot of youth that tell me, "I'm a come to Christ, later, when I'm old. Cause I'm a party!" One kid told me once, "I don't want Jesus to come right now cause I want to get married."

My dear young blood that's reading this book: the song says, "Come, NOW is the time to worship." Even in Spanish we have a song in our Adventist hymnals talking about "Oh, Jóvenes

Venid," that can be translated to "Come, Young People, Come."

Why wait until you're old and tired? God wants to use you now. God used youngsters all throughout the Bible like Shadrach, Meshach, Abednego, Daniel, and David. What are you waiting for?

And the final thing that I like about "Richie Rich" is he came to the right Person. He didn't call those Psychic Networks that used to be promoted on BET all the time with Miss Cleo and Dionne Warwick. He wasn't trying to get jacked for $15.99 a minute. Nope. He came correct, to the Man, Christ Jesus. If you want to find out the final destination to your soul, don't go rent the movie with the same title; don't go to psychics, run to Jesus.

Years ago, I was preaching in New York and somebody told me that in Chinatown, you can get a Louis Vuitton wallet for $5! So Sunday morning before heading to the airport, I asked one of the youth to take me there. Christmas was coming up, so I could knock out four presents with a twenty spot! Or maybe I could sell one of them to a friend for $30 and make a profit! (You know me!)

While I was there, a woman was sitting down, next to a table, reading people's palms. She hissed at me to come over as well. (*Isn't that just like the devil, the snake,* I thought.)

I kind of looked at her with a Bruce Willis smirk and said, "No, thanks. I am a Christian. I don't need no fortune-teller telling me my future. I already know. My God is gonna come back for me, one day pretty soon." She surprised me when she said, "I know you're a Christian."

She knows I'm a Christian? Keep in mind I have a bald head and a goatee. Plus, I had on jean shorts that almost reached my ankles (that could of been mistaken for highwaters) and had on my Nike Air Force 1s with a long white tee with a tank top underneath.

Nowhere in my gear did I have a "What would Jesus do?" logo. How did she know I was a Christian? She said, "I see an angel walking next to you with a sword." Whaaat?! You see an angel next to me with his sword drawn out, and you ain't scared? That sin you are committing is punished by death in the Bible![2] I walked away not giving her the opportunity to answer. I wasn't about to spend any more time talking to Broom-Hilda. I'll holla at Jesus instead.

That's what the rich young ruler did, and he asked Him an important question about the life to come. "Good Teacher, what I gotta do to get hooked up with eternal life?" I remember seeing Michael Jackson in an interview once saying that he wanted to live forever. This young man is basically saying the same thing. How can I live forever?

Jesus didn't answer him right away; instead, He answered him with another question! "Why you calling Me good? Only God is good, bro." Was Jesus asking him a trick question? Because what He was practically saying was, "Why you calling Me God? Only He is good."

I don't think it was a trick question at all. Jesus was handing him the microphone, like telling him, "Mr. Preacha Man, testify. Tell them I'm the Man! Tell them I am God!" But nothing. He didn't say nothing. Only the coquís were heard. I think Jesus wanted him to say,

- "Because God is good, all the time. And all the time, God is good! And You are Him!"
- "Because when You speak, even the winds and the water obey You!"[3]
- "Because I've tasted and seen 'that the LORD is good'!"[4]
- "Because when You give the command, people see dead men walking from their tombs!"

Or at the very least, he should've said like Peter, "Because 'You are the Christ, the Son of the living God'!"[5]

It makes me mad that he didn't say a word. I don't understand why he couldn't have. Every chance I get, I'm on the mic or a magazine or on the radio talking about how good God is.

There's a song that I don't like for nothing. I hear it frequently by the youth before AY. It's kind of whack, to be honest. It says, "What you feel about Jesus? He's alright. What you feel about Jesus? He's dynamite!" Now the dynamite part is pretty cool, but "He's alright"? Yo' mama is alright! Eggplant is alright! And Boca burgers! But Jesus? He's more than alright, people, He's AWESOME! (WARNING! WARNING! Next time a praise and worship team sings that song in front of me, I'm whacking somebody in the head with a Bible! And one of those BIG old school Catholic Bibles too!)

What a missed opportunity. To think he made that great

entrance in vain. Now he becomes shy. I can picture someone in the background screaming out, "Don't be scared!" Rich dude dropped the ball. I can't help but think, what about us? How many times have we dropped it as well? Maybe today at the bus stop, at school, or at work.

Some of us only go to church to feed off the pastor. But when it's time to share the gospel, we don't. Dr. Tony Evans calls that "constipated Christianity"!

I remember when we moved to Florida from Chicago, my mother could've swore she had died and gone to heaven. Those palm trees with the coconuts on them had my moms floating on cloud nine. One day we were cruising in Coral Springs, checking out the big houses, when my mother spots a mansion with a mango tree. She told me to stop the car and go ask if we can have some. "We'll even take the ones on the ground. It don't matter." (Caribbean people are funny. If a mango is rotten on one side, we don't care! We'll cut that part off with a knife and throw it away! Then we'll devour the good side! We'll even eat a green mango with some salt!)

I walked up to the palace—even though I was surprised I made it that far without a security guard shocking me with a stun gun—and knocked on the door. No answer. Then I hear a woman's voice (who sounded like she was hiding) from far away. She said, "What do you want?"

"I'm with my moms and she wants to know if we can have some mangoes from the tree."

"No!" she said, real rudelike. "Not even the ones on the

ground?" I asked patiently. She hollered at me, "I SAID NO! *¿NO HABLES INGLES?* I SAID NO!"

That night I came back at two in the morning and stole twenty-nine mangoes! I looked like a Floridian Santa Claus with a plastic Hefty bag! I even jumped over the gate and broke it! (Keep in mind, that was B.C.—Before Christ!)

We, as well, have a mango of a message (the gospel) that's sweet and juicy, but we also refuse to share it. We have a message of hope, power, and freedom. However, we keep it to ourselves most of the time.

Anyways, since he didn't answer Jesus, Jesus answered him. Because God always answers prayers. Jesus said, "Bro, you know the commandments: Don't kill. Don't be trying to be a playa-playa and mess around on your wifey. Don't be jacking nothing that's not yours. Don't be lying. Don't be cheating people. Respect your pops and your moms."

And then the rich young ruler interrupts Jesus and says, "Hold up, hold up. Bro, I done kept all Your commandments, since I was a little shorty." Can you believe this guy? Not only does he have big pockets, he has a BIG head as well! And did you notice, he said "I" twice? "What 'I' gotta do to get hooked up . . . ?" and " 'I' done kept . . ." It kind of reminds you of a certain angel named Lucifer, doesn't it? He was giving Jesus his credentials. What a snob! Max Lucado says he didn't need a résumé, he needed a Redeemer! We don't need a system, we need a Savior![6]

Aren't we just like him though? We have twenty-eight doctrines—or a list—that tells us we have to stop eating meat in order to be saved. When are we going to stop believing that lie that we will go to heaven because of what we do or stop doing? We will be saved because of what He already did for us, two thousand years ago, on Calvary!

And he was lying when he said he kept all the commandments. So right there, he's sinning! He'd been in the church all his life and thought he was straight. Sometimes that's the problem. He became self-sufficient, even spiritually. How about you? Were you born in the church? You was?! Where, in the back by the baptism pool? Did one of the Dorcas ladies help your mother in labor? You guys are "Jesus freaks," for reals! Pastor Tony Ávila once told me, "I wasn't born in the church; I was born in the hospital!" Ha!

The rich man thought he had it all under control and dared to speak when God was talking. The same God that gave the Ten Commandments to Moses is in his presence, and he cuts Him off. Jesus wasn't finished naming them. He said only five, if you count cheating with lying, and he tells Jesus, "Done that!"

We talk too much sometimes, don't we? And we listen too little. James tells us we should be "quick to listen," and "slow to speak."[7]

Then Jesus looked at him . . . still with love. Even though this dude just told Him that His laws are a piece of cake to follow! Even though he told Jesus, "I got this!" Jesus still loved him, nonetheless. Wow.

We hear preachers all the time saying, "God loves the sinner-man, but hates the sin." And it's true. This is a classic example of that. He loves us, even though.

The prophet Balaam was commissioned to go do some voodoo on the Israelites (God's people) and the Bible says that God still spoke to him![8] I would've karate kicked him in the neck!

When I was working at BK, my homie Ricardo got caught eating a chicken sandwich in the back. The manager looked at him and said, "What are you eating?" "Nothing," he answered, looking all guilty. (Brother had a piece of lettuce stuck on his chin, which looked like he had a green goatee. In fact, he looked like the Grinch that stole Christmas!) He got caught, yet pretended like everything was all good. So did the rich young man.

I don't understand the love of God. But sometimes, I can see His love in events that happen in our everyday life.

When my first niece was born, Ahna Marie, I remember being crazy about her. I bought her first pair of Nikes. She's half white and half Puerto Rican, so I was proud we were going to have a Spanish-speaking Barbie in our fam. One day, I was lifting her up and down in the air and she was laughing. I guess it was tickling her little belly. But I didn't know that her mother gave her some baby food to eat. So, me being ignorant, I kept bouncing her in the air. Like a dummy, I was even singing "I Believe I Can Fly" to her. Then, in slow motion, she vomits IN MY MOUTH! And I had my mouth wide open, looking like Sylvester Stallone saying, "Yo, Adrian!"

Yuck! Split pea soup! Man, I wanted to throw her like a football—a Hail Mary pass! And just when I was about to, she looked at me with an "I just did a boo-boo" look and I looked at her and felt sorry. *Ay, Bendiiito,* I thought. That's my little princess. I can't throw her across the room. I love her. Besides, she has Ramos blood.

That's exactly how Jesus looks at us. And how He looked at "Rick the ruler" that day. He looked at him with love. Even though he just vomited all over God's laws, God looked at him and felt compassion.

Jesus probably thought, *Ay, dito, the money I have given him has made him self-sufficient. Lemme tell him how it is, then, with love.* "Papo, if you wanna be perfect, all you need to do is just one thing: Sell everything you have and give it to the poor. Then I'm a hook you up, don't worry about it."[9]

Wow! Did you catch that? Dude was one sin away from being perfect! All he needed to do is leave that one thing. (I need to stop doing like 985 things!) This guy was close to perfection! All he had to do was give his money to the poor.

Church folk read that and think we have to live in poverty. But no! God doesn't tell you the same thing He'll tell your brother. He treats you as an individual. To one person He might tell to leave pornography. Another, He might say stop smoking. The rich young ruler was about to lose his salvation because of his cheddar, because in his case, "Mo' money, mo' problems!" Finally, Jesus told homie, "When you do all that, come follow Me."

What?! Jesus is telling him to be His thirteenth disciple. He used the same words when He asked Peter, Andrew,

James, and John.[10] Like when He asked Philip,[11] and just like when He asked Levi.[12]

"Sir, it will be an honor to follow You and serve You for the rest of my life." Oh, how I wish he would've said that. He didn't. He walked away sad perhaps mumbling to himself, "I ain't going to sell my Lexus and get a hooptie. No way."

"He loved the gifts of God more than he loved the Giver. . . . He refused the offer of eternal life."[13]

Money was his idol, his god. Though he appeared to have it all, he didn't have jack if he didn't have God. He went out like a sucker. Chilling, isn't it? We know that at least one Seventh-day Adventist is going to be lost when Jesus comes. That could be me or you.

Years ago, I was preaching in Philadelphia and a demon got inside an eight-year-old kid. The final amen was said and people were starting to go home. A father came from the back, bear-hugging his kid and screaming for help. "Willy! Pastor!" he shouted. "Help me! I think my son is possessed!" The people that did stay back after the service now ran out the church so fast, it looked like they stole something!

The father brought the kid to the front next to the pulpit and laid him on the floor. He was holding his son's hands down and the pastor was holding his legs, trying to control him. All I had to do was jump on him! I thought of that old Mortal Kombat video game that says, "Finish him!" and "Fatality."

Before I could act though, the little kid pushed his father on the ground and stood up. He looked over to me and the pastor, and said, "I want to fight you." I looked over to the pastor kind of worried, and said, "Uh . . . he must be talking to you, homie! After all, you're the one that went to school for this!"

Then I remembered I had anointing oil in my pocket that I was going to use on a young lady that asked me to pray over her because she thought she had cancer. While I was taking it out of my pocket, in the midst of bubblegum wrappers and lint, the pastor said to the kid, "You ain't gonna fight Willy or me! You're going up against Jesus, who, by the way, already defeated you with His death on the cross and resurrection!" The pastor then placed his hands over the little man's head and started praying. Then he started saying Psalm 23 in Spanish. I repeated it in English in case it was a bilingual demon! (I joke around with this story, but really it ain't no laughing matter when you're caught up in the middle of this great controversy between God and His angels, and the devil and his.)

I was about to put oil on the kid's head when his father got up from the ground. I was concentrating on the boy, so it kind of startled me and I splashed his father instead! Then his moms came running inside the church and she got it as well. I remembered that old commercial that had a Spanish mom saying, *"Con Mazola, no estas sola."* Then I put some on the eight-year-old. He started screaming, and my hand started moving like I was break-dancing, doing the wave! Then he fell on the ground. And in the name of Jesus, the little kid returned to normal, with a bunch of elders surrounding him and all of us feeling exhausted.

The parents took him home and the pastor took me to my

hotel. "Pastor," I asked, "how can a demon possess an eight-year-old boy?"

We later found out that in their house, they watched all kinds of worldly movies and listened to worldly music. It's crazy because we put locks on our doors and alarms on our cars, yet we fail to "guard well the avenues of the soul."[14] That day, the mother threw out everything that would allow Satan access into their lives and in their kid's life. And we should do the same.

What is He telling you to throw out? What is that "one thing" that's a stumbling block from you giving your life fully over to Jesus?

---

1. Max Lucado, *Just Like Jesus,* 3.
2. Leviticus 20:27.
3. See Luke 8:25.
4. Psalm 34:8.
5. Matthew 16:16.
6. Max Lucado, *Cast of Characters,* 189.
7. James 1:19.
8. Numbers 22:12.
9. See Matthew 19:21.
10. Matthew 4:19–22.
11. John 1:43.
12. Luke 5:27.
13. Ellen G. White, *The Desire of Ages,* 520.
14. Ellen G. White, *Messages to Young People,* 285.

CHAPTER EIGHT

SCREENPLAY

There I was, without the backup of my homeboys, in the middle of a bad neighborhood at night, and a stranger had just threatened me. He said they had me surrounded. Was it in retaliation for the sins of my past? Was it a gang thing, or a stickup? None of the above. I was about to go face-to-face with . . . a fallen angel.

I was in Virginia, waiting for my ride back to the hotel after a church meeting. I was with three church sisters that I had met the night before. I was exhausted, to be honest. I really didn't wanna be there. I would've rather been in my room, sleeping or watching TV, because I had just finished preaching. (I don't know about other preachers, but I used to work at a metal company and for reals, the forty-five minutes that I take to preach a sermon tires me more than working ten hours at the factory. I use every fiber of my being when I'm in the pulpit. I try to give God my 100 percent when I'm on the mic. I use mental, spiritual, and physical effort and a lot of emotions. It's warfare up there. Besides, I don't think God will settle for anything less. Speaking of spiritual warfare, check out the bizarre thing that happened to me that night.)

We were cleaning up the gymnasium of a public high school that we had rented for that weekend. The elders had asked me if I could stay with the three lovely ladies from the praise and worship team while they took the folding chairs back to the church because I didn't fit in the car. I kidded around with them and made fun of my weight. "I don't fit in nobody's car, to be honest. People drive me around in the back of U-Hauls." They started laughing and I agreed to stay with the sisters.

The guys took off and the girls and I started chitchatting. From afar, we saw the shadow of a man that was kind of blocking the brightness of a streetlight. We paid him no mind, figuring that he was probably somebody that was just passing by.

The girls were trying to convince me to go bowling when the dude walked straight to us. He asked, "What would you tell a friend if he thinks God don't forgive him?" One of the girls, Janene, told him that God forgives anybody that asks for forgiveness, no matter what they've done. I agreed with her and told him to tell his friend about Paul, who was basically an assassin for the Sanhedrin, and about David, an adulterer, and about Moses, who also killed a man but who today is in the company of angels in heaven because of God's grace.

He said, "Thank you," then walked away. I felt proud of myself and my ego got the best of me. I thought, *Yes! One more star for my crown!*

I resumed my bowling conversation with the girls and even threatened them that they don't want none of me. I lied and told them that they used to call me "Twinkle Toes Flintstone" when I was in a league.

That's when the dude walked back up to us and said, "What if that somebody is me? I don't think God forgives me . . ." He started crying. Janene hugged him. That made him cry harder. So I motioned for her to let me take over. I told him that if God forgave a piece of junk like me, that he had nothing to worry about.

He said, "God don't forgive me." I said, "Yes, He does, homeboy. Man, the devil done lied to you." I told him. There was a song out by Laura Story called "Mighty to Save" at that time, so I reminded him of that.

But every good thing I was telling him only made him feel worse. Dude was foaming at the mouth and running at the nose. Now he wasn't crying; brotha was wailing hard. He said, "God don't forgive me," a second time. But this time, he sounded different. His eyes rolled back in his head and I stood there in shock, not believing what was happening. I would've run, to be honest, but I think one of the girls had me in a leglock!

I bear-hugged him tight as he started roaring louder. The two other girls, Luz and Vanessa, got on their knees and started praying. Janene joined them. Keep in mind, they had on dresses and they were kneeling on the concrete! Yo, they some prayer warriors, for reals!

Demon dude did a Matrix! His back started bending like

a plastic spoon as his head hit the floor. I leaned forward as well and my hands touched my toes. And man, you can take the kid out the ghetto, but you can't take the ghetto out the kid, cause all I can think was, *Yo, I just did a sit-up! Now if I can only get rid of these love handles!*

I told him, "God is gonna save you, but you need to want it. You need to accept His forgiveness! In fact, cry out to Him right now and tell Him to save you! Say, 'God save me!' "

He said it with no problem, but the situation just kept getting crazier. He even started twisting up like a pretzel. I'm thinking to myself, *Lord, he's asking You to save him. Why don't You?* The Holy Spirit whispered in my ear, *"It's because he's calling another god, not Me."*

He was saying, "god, save me," with a lowercase *g*! No wonder nothing was happening. It reminded me of the sailors who were crying out to their "own god"[1] in the book of Jonah and the violent storm still raged on. He needed to ask God to save him in the name of Jesus. This time I raised my voice, "Say, 'Jesus, save me!' " He said, "I said, 'God, save me!' " "No, be specific," I shouted. "Name your God! Say, 'Jesus!' "

That's when he looked at me like he wanted to kill me. "We have you surrounded," he threatened. When he said that, I immediately got a vision of me doing one of those secret sins that nobody knows about, just a few weeks before.

I knew Satan was messing with me. The devil will mess with you and bring up your past. I should've brought up his future and stuck my tongue out at him. This wasn't just some dude walking the streets; I was up against a supernatural force. That night he also said, "Beware of Anime! Beware of Anime!" (Japanese cartoons that often have violence or sexually explicit content.)

I screamed out to the girls to pray for him, that I was gonna pray for myself! Then I opened up my Bible and started reading Psalm 91. I reminded him that God's angels have His children surrounded[2] and not even a legion of them can match the power of Jesus.[3] He finally calmed down and he cried out to the Lord, "JESUS, save me!"

And just like that, he stood still. I looked at him with a "stop playing" look on my face. I was exhausted. So was he. "You straight now?" I asked. "Yeah," he said. "Thank you. Jesus saved me . . . I'm hungry." It sounded good to me. "Let's go get him something to eat." I thought, *I can sure use a Scooby Snack myself.*

As I think back to that night, I'm reminded of all the other gods in our lives. Like money, music, celebrities, etc. The Bibles says, "If serving the LORD seems undesirable to you, then choose for yourselves this day whom will you serve, whether the gods your forefathers served beyond the River, or the gods of the Amorites, in whose land you are living. But as for me and my household, we will serve the LORD."[4]

I'm wondering, Who is your god? Who's your daddy? Who have you signed a contract with to sit in the director's chair, to make the movie of your life? Jesus or Satan?

When Tupac Shakur died, Marlon Wayans said, "Tupac was the most awesome character that God has ever written."

And I thought to myself, *Wow, what an awesome thing to say about somebody.* But it's not true. God is not writing our story. We are! However, God will direct it if we let Him.

I wrote a screenplay like three months ago called, "To Catch a Thief." It's a gangsta-flick (based on a true story) about a gang of thieves called The 4 Horsemen. One of the four gives his life to Jesus at the end. I've already sent it out to Tyler Perry, Mel Gibson's Icon Productions, and to the directors of *Fireproof.* If nobody calls, I plan to film it myself, straight-up bootleg-style from a cell phone camera if I have to! I'm trying to make it, cuz!

I even gave myself a part in the movie, cause I have been trying to become an actor since back in the day! My brother and I had small parts in movies shot in South Florida and we've been in *CSI: Miami.* I even introduced The Rock in his biography called *The People's Champ.* Mostly extras stuff, though.

But for my movie, I gave myself one of the lead rolls. Because I refuse to be an extra in a movie that I wrote! This can be my one and only shot!

Right now, everybody is writing the screenplay of their lives, spiritually speaking. The New International Version of the Bible says it like this: "We have been made a spectacle to the whole universe, to angels as well as to men."[5] Eugene Peterson puts it this way: "God has put us who bear his Message on stage in a theatre. . . . We're something everyone stands around and stares at, like an accident in the street."[6] The whole UNIVERSE is watching how we live our lives!

SCREENPLAY

Some of us are living a comedy or a romantic comedy. Some of us got so much drama going on that it can only be labeled as that. A lot of us are living both—a dramedy.

Some are rated "PG." And some of our lives are filled with violence, nudity, and vulgarity, classifying them as "R" rated. I want my life to be rated "E" for everyone. Just like Jesus' life was. Parents even brought their shorties to check Him out.[7]

People tell me all the time, "Your ministry is good to reach a certain type of people." No, it's not! My ministry needs to be able to reach everyone. I've seen Jewish dudes, mothers, gangstas, inmates, and business people cry when I allowed God to direct me on the pulpit.

What is your movie rated? Is it rated "G" only when you are in church? Are you living *la vida loca*? Are there deleted scenes in your life that only you, God, and the angels know about? Is Satan sitting in the director's chair? If he is, do like Donald Trump and tell him, "You're fired!"

It's time for us to bring God back into the picture. He wants to make a masterpiece out of you. And the good news is that not only is He an awesome Director, but He is also an Editor.

My brother and I have been filmed in a bunch of movies, but we hardly ever came out in any one of them. For whatever reason, we ended up on the "editing room floor." That's the same thing that will happen with our sins if we let Jesus direct the screenplay of our lives. Yeah, "the wages of sin is death"[8] and we all deserve to die, but God has provided an "alternate ending" in His "Director's Cut" of our lives.

I was in a movie like ten years ago with Eva Mendes and Ice-T called *The Disciples*. The movie was so whack that the director removed himself from the project! Now if you do a Google search on that film, you will see that it was directed by Alan Smithee. But Alan Smithee is the fake name or the pseudonym designated by the Directors Guild of America to replace the actual names of directors who wish not to be credited for a particular film. The original directors don't want nothing to do with the films. Even though they worked hard filming the movie, they don't like the way it turned out for one reason or another.

The same thing is going to happen when Jesus comes. Satan is not gonna want anything to do with the lost. (He's just like a disgruntled employee that quits his job angrily and comes back to kill everyone in the building.) Therefore, those that are lost will be labeled by Satan like a film shot by Alan Smithee.

But not only will God's archenemy do this, God will do it also. When it's all said and done, God will say sadly to those unfortunate who didn't let Him direct their lives, "I never knew you. Away from me, you evildoers!"[9] Wow. There you have it. Even Jesus will brand those unfortunate an Alan Smithee film!

One day real soon, Steven Spielberg, Ron Howard, George Lucas, and Quentin Tarantino will all bow down and call Jesus, "Lord." Whether they like it or not!

But the choice is ours. Come Judgment Day, when all the redeemed are gathered and the "Academy Award" is given for the "Best Director," who will win the prize? Again I ask you, who will you choose to direct the movie of your life? Jesus or Satan?

Imagine that day when the angel Gabriel is walking up to the podium to announce the winner, while the drums roll in the background: "And the winner is . . ."

Totally up to you.

---

1. Jonah 1:4–6.
2. 2 King 6:16, 17.
3. Luke 8:30–35.
4. Joshua 24:15.
5. 1 Corinthians 4:9.
6. 1 Corinthians 4:9–13, *The Message.*
7. Matthew 19:13.
8. Romans 6:23,
9. Matthew 7:23.

CHAPTER NINE

"HAVE YOU CONSIDERED MY SERVANT?"

Somebody once told me, "Your test can become your testimony; your mess can become your message; and your misery can end up being your ministry." Man! That stuck to my heart like me sittin' in one of those little seats at the Miami Arena—really stuck! Back when I first started my ministry, Satan wanted to bring me down and tried to use a girl to do it. I look at it like the story of Job.

One day the angels came to present themselves before the Lord, and Satan also came with them.[1]

The Lord: Where have you come from?

Satan: You know me. I've just been "chillin' like a villain."

The Lord: Have you considered My servant, Willy Ramos?

Satan (laughing): Ha! Willy Ramos?! The Ghetto Preacher?! What are You, kidding? You jokin', right?

The Lord: Do I look like a stand-up comedian to you? Do I look like one of the Wayans brothers to you? Yes, Willy Ramos.

Satan: Oh, my bad. But are You sure? Willy Ramos has no willpower! He has no self-control or discipline. In fact, show him a ninety-nine cent Whopper commercial and he'll break his diet! Willy Ramos is a piece of cake!

Meanwhile, my fat self is on earth thinking, *Duh, did somebody say "cake"?*

Satan: Alright, then, I'm a "consider" Your boy Willy Ramos, but he's gonna curse You to Your face. Just watch!

The Lord: Very well, then. You can take everything he has is in his hands, but on the man himself, do not lay a finger.

Then Satan goes out from the presence of the Lord[2] and got inside his lowrider 1964 Chevy Impala with 16 switches. He put on the new Eminem CD and started the car. All of a sudden, he's surrounded by demons.

Legion: Yo, yo, yo, we heard you were gonna go tempt Willy Ramos. You need help?

Satan: Nah, bro, it's Willy. I got him. You all just worry about tempting every single young kid that Willy preaches to. Tempt them with music, movies, drugs, and sex. And kill them if you can. I'll take care of this punk they call "The Ghetto Preacher."

4GVN

A haunting piano music is heard in the background.

While that was taking place, I was at a Camp Kulaqua in High Springs, Florida, giving my testimony to six hundred jóvenes. (God used me powerfully that night.) When I finished, we all went to the gym where Pastor Alvin Payne and his Playground Ministries were gonna have some recreational activities. Then I saw her. One of the most beautifulest (I know it's not a word, it just sounds cool!) girl I have ever seen in my life. She walked up to me and introduced herself as "Princesa." (Names have been changed to protect the innocent.)

Willy: Nice to meet you, Princesa. My name is . . . Bond. James Bond. (Just kidding. But I always wanted to say that!) My name is Willy Ramos.

Princesa: I know who you are. Everybody knows Willy.

Ooooh, I felt cool. "Pop the collar, pop the collar." I felt like that character that used to be on CBS', *Everybody Loves Raymond.* To make the long story short, I asked for her phone number, and she gave it to me. Yeees! I was very much attracted to her and she appeared to be interested. She lived four hours away from me so I knew that our relationship was gonna be mainly over the phone, being that I didn't have a car at the time. Keep in mind, this was like ten years ago, before I had a laptop and before these long distance deals that cell phone companies now have. So I was paying $360 a month on the phone bill. $360! That wasn't a phone bill, that was like paying rent! But I didn't care. I was falling in love with her. I would send her flowers. Teddy bears. Half-eaten boxes of chocolate. (Wink. Wink.) Love letters. Poetry, like: "My life without you is empty . . . like church on Wednesday nights!" (See, I told you I used that line.) She had a one-year-old son at the time, so I would send him lil' T-shirts and toys. I even gave her a crown once in a glass memorabilia case with an engraving that said, "You will always be my princess."

Things were going awesome. We wrote and called each other for like a year. Then her moms, who was youth director at the time, asked me if I wanted to preach at her church. Immediately, I said, "Yes. Wherever God will send me!" Especially to see my "boo-boo bear."

I went there with the intentions of asking her to be my girlfriend. We'd been talking to each other for months but we still hadn't made anything official.

So I preached at her church. Everything went well. It was one of the most wonderful weekends of my life. Life couldn't of have gotten any better. I was floating on cloud nine. Then it was time for me to leave. I checked out of the motel in the morning, stopped at the corner store, bought her a rose, and headed for her crib to ask her to be my girlfriend.

I knocked at the door, and her father answered.

Willy: What's up, *suegro*? (I tried to give him dap, but he didn't know how to do it. He's old school!) Yo, can I say "Bye" to Princesa?

Princesa's father: *Seguro.* Of course. She's in her room sleeping. You can go in there.

Willy: I can go in there? (Wow. This Christian stuff is great. If he only knew of what a sick pervert I used to be!)

I walked quietly in the room, and tapped her on her shoulders.

Willy *(whispering):* Princesa . . . Princesa. (She wakes up scared, as if she had just seen a monster.) It's only me! It's me, Willy. Hi, baby.

Princesa *(smiling):* Heeey. (I would've asked her how she slept, but one day I asked one of the youth from the church that question and he told me, "Horizontally." Smart aleck.)

Willy: Listen, I'm about to head back home but I wanna ask you a question. We've been talking for almost a year now and well, I wanted to know if you want to be my . . . uh . . . (I pictured Rob Schneider saying, "You can dooooo it!") . . . girlfriend?

(It was nerve-wracking. I swear I could've wrote a sequel to *The Day the Earth Stood Still.* Because that's exactly what happened. Everything was in slow motion. I could hear my heartbeat.)

Princesa: Willy, my parents love you a lot. In fact, they want me to marry you. (I was like, yeah, I'm in there like swimwear!) My church family loves you. They want you to preach here again. And my son, he adores you. (He adores me? He must think I'm Barney or something! Especially when I have on my purple suit! Dang! And I thought I looked like T. D. Jakes!)

Princesa: And I love you, a lot. (Yeeees!) But . . . (Noooo! Me and that *but* word don't get along for nothing. I thought she was gonna tell me that I was too ghetto.) . . . But . . . But you are too fat. (Too "fat"?! Wow! Obviously, the lil' Babylonian wasn't fully converted! My heart sank quicker than the *Titanic.* I could hear Celine Dion singing in the background!)

Willy: Too fat?

Princesa: Yes, Willy. You are too fat. I mean, my father is chubby but you are humongous. People are going to call us "El Gordo y La Flaca." (The two hosts of a Spanish program on Univision by the same title that means "fatso and skinny.") Or they are gonna call us Timon and Pumbaa from *The Lion King.* (For a second, I pictured myself singin' "When I was a young warthog.")

Princesa: Willy, believe me, baby, I tried loving you. But I can't.

Willy: Come on, even the Nutty Professor got Jada Pinkett in the end! And so did the Hunchback of Notre Dame! I know I'm fat! But you have never gave me one Jenny Craig hint or nothing! I thought you were likin' me for my heart. Please tell me that you're kidding!

(I thought Ashton Kutcher was gonna pop up from under her bed and say, "You have just got punk'd!" I was mad. I wanted to pillow fight her! I prayed silently, *Lord, remember in the Bible the earth opened up and swallowed some dudes alive?*[3] *Can we have an encore presentation of that?*

I could've dissed her back. I'm from the streets! I got plenty of comebacks! I could've said something like, "First of all, you ain't in no position to crack, cause you just woke up, mamita, and your breath is kicking like Jackie Chan! And you got green stuff coming out your eyes! Eww . . . and, look at your toes! They all jacked up! Go put on some tube socks or something! At least put on some cool Nike ones with the swoosh on them. Yuck!"

But I couldn't say nothing like that. Because the sun was hitting her face from the window and to be honest, she looked like an angel. Yeah, a fallen angel! How dare her!

I was heartbroken. But I wasn't going down without a fight. I got on one knee and begged her!)

Willy: Pleeease. Please, be my girlfriend.
Princesa (*shaking her head*): Nooo. But we can still . . . be friends. (I hate when girls say that! I thought of the movie *Child's Play.* "Hi, I'm Chucky. I'm your friend 'til the end. Hidy-ho.")

Willy: No! I can't be your friend! I don't want you to call me one day and say, "Hi. Guess what? I just met the cutest guy at the mall." That's gonna hurt me a lot. I mean, I wanna be your friend, but gimme some time. After all, I'm trying to be a Christian. Unlike somebody I know. (I took off crying. I got in the car and headed back home to Fort Lauderdale. I've lost homies before and have had relatives die, but on the real, this was more painful than anything I had ever faced. I put on a CD by one of my favorite Christian singers, Junior Kelly Marchena. I started listening to one of his songs that says, *"Dios siempre comprende tus lágrimas."* That means God always understands your tears. I started crying harder. Man, the last time I cried this much, I was on a diet and had just passed a McDonald's in my car!)

That's when Satan tried to take advantage. All of a sudden, I hear that scary tune from the movie *Jaws.*

Satan: Hey, yo, Will. What is that whack song you're listening to? God don't understand your tears. He doesn't know what it feels like to fall in love or have a broken heart. He cannot relate. (And in a voice deeper than James Earl Jones, he says to me, "Come with me, and join the dark side.") I'll give you fame and fortune. And I'll hook you up with Victoria's Secret models, that'll make Princesa look like Ugly

Betty! You don't need her. And you don't need God. What's your favorite Bible quote?

Willy: Delight yourself in the Lord, and He will give you the desires of your heart.

(That was my first mistake. You don't talk to the devil. Never. When Satan knocks on your door, you say, "Jesus, can You answer the door for me?")

Satan: So Psalm 37:4, right? Well, you have delighted yourself in the Lord since you've been baptized and He hasn't gave you the desires of your heart! You wanted Princesa and He didn't give you her! He's a liar. Turn in your badge, bro. I'm a hook you up.

(And just when I was starting to believe him and doubt God's Word, I heard God's voice from heaven in the form of a Superhero: "Here I come to save the day!")

Jesus: Hey, Willy, what's up? First of all, what are you doin' listening to this loser? He is the father of lies![4] Second of all, of course I understand your pain. And of course I know what it feels like to fall in love. Willy, do you know what Matthew 27:27–31 says?

Willy (*embarrassed*): Ummm . . . nope.

Jesus: Well, that's when the Roman soldiers were beating Me up and making fun of Me. They also spit on Me and baseball-batted Me with a stick. Then they took Me and crucified Me.

Satan: So! That doesn't mean that You've been in love! What does that have to do with anything?

Jesus: Everything. That's love in the form of action. Willy, I know that you know what John 3:16 says.

Willy: Sure, everybody does. "For God so loved the world that He gave us His only Son, for whoever believes in . . ."

Jesus: Say that again!

Willy: Say what? "For God so love the world . . ."

Jesus: One more time.

Willy: "For God so love the world . . ."

Jesus: Did you hear what you just said? You said that My Father LOVED the world so much that He sent Me to die instead of You.

(My boy, Pastor Freddy Rodriguez, once said in a sermon, "Jesus wasn't killed by the Jews! Jesus wasn't killed by Roman soldiers! And Jesus wasn't killed by Judas or Pilate! Nope! Jesus was killed by His Father cause He LOVED us so much! He'd rather have His Son die, in order for us to live . . . and live forever! Now that's love!")

Jesus: You see, We know what love is, Willy. I am love. I even accepted the mission and came and died for you and everyone else. I know what it feels like to be rejected. My own people rejected Me. And a broken heart? I know what that feels like too. After all, that was the cause of My death.[5] (He hugged me.) Wilito, you know those flowers you used to give Princesa? Well, I give you flowers every day. Just look outside. You know the little love letters you used to write her? Well, I wrote you the ultimate love letter, the Bible. And you know that crown that you gave Princesa in that glass memorabilia case that you bought at K-Mart? (Uh . . . *shhhh* . . . Lord, I didn't want nobody to know that part.) Well, I'm a give you a crown of life[6] when you make it to heaven despite all the obstacles that Satan put in front of you. You need to hang in there, papo. I love you, little homie. You gonna make it. I'm a see you through this. I gotta another plan for you that does not involve Princesa. I'm a hook you up nice. Watch. Take my hands and trust Me.

(Did Jesus just call me "little"? He really knows how to make me feel good! I took Him by the hands that day, then told the devil off.)

Willy: Satan, I rebuke you in the name of Jesus of Nazareth! "Hit the road Jack and don't you come back, no more, no more, no more, no more!"

(Satan, embarrassed and defeated, left my sight for a season but before he did, he said the immortal words of Arnold Schwarzenegger in *The Terminator*.)

"HAVE YOU CONSIDERED MY SERVANT?"

Satan: "I'll be back."

(Princesa ended up leaving the church. And goin' to clubs and drinking. So I know, now, why things happened the way it did. But today, she is married with three kids and got re-baptized. In fact, we are good friends. And me, I got married as well, to the most prettiest girl in the whole wide world and have adopted her son. I am a happy man. And I still preach the everlasting gospel of Jesus. God is awesome!)

The Lord blessed the latter part of Willy's life more than the first.[7]

Today, I no longer grab Jesus by the hands. I have Him in a headlock! And I smile sometimes as I'm reminded that through perseverance, even the turtle reached the ark. So if you're getting tested today by the enemy, and if your life is a mess and full of misery, you have to hang in there! I can't wait to see the ministry that God has in store for you.

"Hang in there. The alternative to that is to let go. And, to let go is . . . hell." - Pastor Juan Rodriguez

1. Job 1:6.
2. Job 1:12.
3. Numbers 16:31–33.
4. John 8:44.
5. Ellen G. White, *The Desire of Ages,* 772.
6. Revelation 2:10.
7. Job 42:12.

CHAPTER TEN

"WHAT SHALL I DO, THEN, WITH JESUS?"

I stood there, still, like a kid playing Freeze Tag. Four hoodlums in a car just flashed a double-barrel shotgun at me. Should I have run? Nope. Because I can't run fast. (The only time you'll ever see me running is chasing after an ice cream truck! "I just want a popsicle! I ain't gonna jack you, I swear!") Should I have prayed? Yeah, maybe I should have. But at that time I didn't have a relationship with Jesus and I didn't want to feel like a punk, calling Him then, when I was scared.

I closed my eyes, and saw my life flash in front of me. I saw a bunch of restaurant logos. How sad. *Maybe I SHOULD pray,* I thought. *After all, I have nothing to lose, but . . . MY LIFE!* I said, "Jesus, if You get me out of this mess, I'm a start going to ALL the churches in Florida, from this day forward."

It was ten o'clock at night and my moms had just finished calling me to come inside. I had a ten o'clock curfew back then. Nowadays, kids are getting ready at ten to go out! Go figure. My mother yelled out my name, "WILLY!" but I ignored her cause I was hanging with the boys in the hood at the corner. Around ten fifteen, my mother called me a second time. This time she called me "WILLIAM!" And the earth shook a little.

Now, I don't know about your mama, but when my mama called me by all fifteen of my names, that's when I knew I was in trouble! ("William Ramos Maldonado Cruz Otero Delatorre Santana Montana Capone Corleone Pacino De Niro Brigante Garcia Smith!") Especially if she's watching telenovelas. Don't you dare interrupt a Hispanic mom while she's watching *Betty La Fea*! You'll get beat down! Wait until a commercial break.

My mama was gangsta. She wore Dickies and everything. My mama used to whip me with phone cords! My skin would swell up so much, people thought I had jailhouse tattoos. My moms wasn't like these new school mothers that don't know how to raise their kids so they ask Supernanny. My moms will drop-kick Supernanny, then put her in an anklelock and make her want to tap out! Moms was hardcore. And she's just a short little fat lady that looks like Happy Feet and smells like Raid!

Mothers nowadays always want to ground their kids. We didn't get grounded; we got pounded! Sometimes my moms made us go outside, grab a tree branch, and take off the leaves so she can whoop us with it! Hispanic and black mothers must've went to the same beating school, because a lot of my friends tell me their mothers did the same to them. The "switch" is more feared in the hood than the Bloods and the Crips put together! Rumor has it George Bush told President

Obama to search every ghetto in America for weapons of mass destruction!

Kids nowadays threaten their parents with calling the cops. My moms would be like, "Yeah, call the cops! But I'm a choke you before they get here!"

And you can forget about "time-outs." My mama don't even know what that means! That's when she pulls out the "Me no speako English" card. I heard a comedian say once, "We didn't have time-out, we had lights out!" Bang! TKO! I honestly think my mama could've beat up Mike Tyson in his prime!

Let me stop before any police officer that's reading this book decides to issue a warrant for my mama's arrest. I'd feel sorry for the prison population. My mama will shank an inmate! She's a roughneck! But she did all that out of love. And I still turned out bad—imagine if she didn't hit me! My personal opinion is a nice little spank in the behind, to keep your kids in line, is a good remedy for these knucklehead kids who now walk the earth with no respect whatsoever.

Anyways, a little later that night, around ten thirty-five—because God always sends a prophet to warn His people before He strikes—my little sister Cuca yelled for me to come home. "Willy, you gonna get in troouble!" So I finally said, "Peace out," to my homies and headed home. I didn't want another chancleta footprint on my hand or leg.

As I walked to my apartment complex, I noticed the neighborhood drug dealer, Fat Bubba, in front of me. We were neighbors and he was walking to his house as well. Or limping to his house. Gangstas don't walk, they limp. Even if their legs ain't hurting! He had a silk shirt like was in style back then (that you bought at the flea market for $3), cutoff corduroy shorts, Converses, and a pager that only doctors had at the time. (Two years later, I got one the size of a VCR. People would rent at Blockbuster and try to put it on my hip!)

I started to walk a little faster because I wanted to get his attention. I wanted to be down with the neighborhood king-pin. (I remember Ray Liotta in the movie *Goodfellas,* said, "As far as I remember, I always wanted to be a gangster." And so did I.)

As I got like three steps behind him, I saw this Cadillac (one of those big ones, like in *Donnie Brasco*) driving slow with the lights off. I thought to myself, *DRIVE-BY!* But I froze up. I couldn't move. Four ruffians in the car is enough to paralyze anybody (They looked like they were trained to fight by Apollo Creed because they all had "the eye of the tiger"!), especially if one of them had a sawed-off shotgun.

They passed me by and I could tell that they weren't after me—they were going to kill my neighbor. I wanted to warn him but I couldn't. My mouth was sealed shut. (You can tell I was scared cause it's hard for a Puerto Rican to stay quiet!) I wanted to scream, but nothing was coming out. Not a "hum-n-a, hum-n-a, hum-n-a" like Jackie Gleason or nada. Not even like in the movies when they scream out, "Loook ouuut!" in slow motion.

Anyways, it was already too late. While I was working up

my courage to speak, one of the thugs was hanging out the passenger seat window with the gun right next to Fat Bubba's face.

Now a shotgun shoots different from a pistol or a rifle. It shoots out hundreds of little buckshots. It splatters everywhere. Three people can get shot even though you're only aiming at one. And I was so close to my neighbor that I would've got smoked as well. You know what I did? Man, I hit the floor so fast I looked like Free Willy jumping over that little white kid! I looked like a 747 going down! (Somebody shouted, "Mayday! Mayday!" Kids thought I was a bounce house. They started jumping all over me . . .) I landed inside some bushes and the earth shook again. Between me and my mama, you would swear we were living in California!

Now, even though I was hiding out, I'm Latino. And we are nosey. We love drama. We don't want to get killed, but we don't mind seeing the fireworks. So I stuck my head out, real slow like. I looked like a fat ostrich!

As I peeked out, I saw Bubba with his arms stretched out and he said, "Do it, dawg. Cause if you don't do it, I'm a blast you later."

Do it? Whaaat?! Was this guy fearless or just plain dumb? Either way, he was insane in the membrane like Cypress Hill, or he had a death wish like Charles Bronson.

I honestly don't know what happened that night, because the thug with the gun said, "I'll catch you on the rebound, cuz." He got back inside the car and they took off. Maybe he got scared. Or maybe he saw an angel of the Lord protecting Bubba. Or me. Who knows?

Fat Bubba put his arms down like nothing ever happened and walked back to his crib with a gangsta limp. Me? I ran home as fast as I could, talking about "Feet don't fail me now!" Straight to the bathroom too!

As I sat there, looking at the sticker burrs stuck to the fat shoelaces of my suede PUMAs, I said to myself, "Man, I almost died tonight."

I sure wasn't ready. I wanted to get married. I wanted to have kids. (Imagine my kids looking like fat little penguins running around the crib.) I wanted to become an actor or a rapper. I wasn't ready spiritually, either. My parents were Adventists, but I wasn't. I had left the church. (I didn't even know what the word *Adventist* meant. Some of our youth don't even know either. They don't even know how to say it! "I'm Seventh-day A-dentist." A-dentist?! I tell them to hook me up! My wisdom tooth has been killing me!)

Was God trying to get my attention and tell me to come back? I think He was. So you know what I did? That night, I rededicated my life to God, right there in the bathroom. And I started visiting all the churches in South Florida, just like I promised. I've been to Church's Chicken in Miami, Church's Chicken in Fort Lauderdale, and Church's Chicken in Orlando. I'm a man of my word . . .

Shortly after that night, I got re-baptized. Ten years later, I married a princess I met on MySpace when she requested me as a friend. (Though she won't admit that now because it's all about Facebook!) And I am helping her raise her six-year-old son, who the other day almost made me cry when he asked, "Can I call you 'Papi'?" When I was just dating Lynette, a lot of people said, "Why are you going to hook up with a girl that has extra baggage?" But I don't look at it that way. I consider myself blessed. Wow, God has considered me worthy with trusting me with this little kid and helping his mother take him to heaven. They are both welcome to be a part of my space, forever.

I also have a Christian rap CD out, and have a screenplay that's ready to be made into a movie. And I'm a published author. And I went back and got my high school diploma at the age of thirty-five. Not bad for a street punk, huh? I refuse to be another statistic. I am living my dream. I'm ready, now. That doesn't mean I don't slip from time to time, though.

Like Mick Foley—the greatest hardcore wrestler ever, in my opinion—once said, "Sometimes I'm like that little engine that could. I think I can, I think I can. But sometimes I just don't know." What I do know is that if something were to happen to me right now, I am ready to meet my Maker. And I know now that I won't get to heaven because of what I do, but because of what He did for me.

What about you? As you are reading the last chapter of this book, and we live out the last chapters of human history, can you honestly say that you are ready for the second advent of the Messiah, Christ Jesus? When you think about His return, does it make you happy or give you chills? Have you added Water to the empty bottle of your life? Are you in desperate need of a Savior? Who's directing your screenplay? Is Jesus your Co-Pilot?

Before handing Jesus over to die, Pilate said, "What shall I do, then, with Jesus who is called Christ?"[1] Wow. What a question. How about you? After reading this book, what are you going to do with this Jesus character? When you put this book down, are you going to start living for God, or walk away sad like the rich young ruler?

I'm a very loyal individual. In the streets, I was committed. I would go to jail or die for a band of brothers. The United States Marines has a motto similar to what I'm talking about. They say *"Semper Fi,"* or *"Semper Fidelis."* Which is Latin for "Always Faithful."

In fact, if I was in the military serving in the Middle East, but got caught and became a prisoner of war and they were interrogating me for some top secrets, I don't think I'd ever give in, even if they were torturing me. I guess it's that "never rat on your friends" mentality that they teach us in the hood.

They won't get a word out of me—unless they do ONE thing to me: I have a fear of one thing that if used against me, I'd probably sing like a canary. I fear this thing more than anything on this earth. You want to know what it is? DIETS! (Just kidding. Even though it's half true.)

I fear giant cockroaches. Those big ol' palmetto bugs that fly. Yuck. Little roaches, I don't fear. We had so many of them in the ghetto, I knew half of them by name. I'd leave food out for them on purpose. We were homies! But the big roaches that fly make me freak out! I had my son take a broom and kill one for me not long ago while his mom was on top of the couch screaming. I pretended I was using the bathroom. Really, I was hiding inside the tub! I ain't playing!

Man, one day I was using the bathroom and took off my shirt cause it was hot. I started reading *Insight* magazine and from out of nowhere, a big ol' giant cockroach that looked like the one from *Monsters vs. Aliens* flew onto my head! I think that's why I shave my head bald now. I'm still traumatized! That roach wouldn't let go. It was swinging from my hair like a black Tarzan!

I ran out the bathroom naked! I stopped, dropped, and rolled! My sisters thought I was on fire! I'm scared of those jokers! Let Tony Montana "bury those cockroaches"! I don't even want to see them.

Even typing about it makes me uneasy. I'm looking over my shoulders now, like if somebody's after me.

Well, anyways, if the enemy had me hostage and asked me to give up top secrets, I wouldn't—unless they brought out a jar with a bunch of giant roaches. Then I'll turn state's evidence. I'm a rat on everyone, like Henry Hill! "I think Obama's grandma is a Muslim! And Bill Clinton is a pervert!" I'm a snitch everybody out!

Most of us are willing to die for Jesus. I asked that once in a church and more than half of the congregation raised their hands. But I'm a give you a harder challenge: Why not try living for Him, instead?

To die in Christ is gain.[2] Because the next person we see when we open our eyes is our guardian angel, getting ready to take us home.

But to live for Christ is the hard part; to live for Him when we're discouraged, or hurt, or tired. To live for Him and remain faithful, even when Satan scares you with the cockroaches in your life. That's when you know what's up.

Your friends—or society in general—are going to tell you, "Life is short, you have to live it." Yeah, but live it in fear of the Lord and you will live it forever in the kingdom of heaven!

My boy, David Bracetti, once said in a sermon, "Christ is going to come back, whether you're ready or not." God is going to let you do what you want, though. He won't violate your free will. He will warn you and love you and bless you, but He won't choose for you. You have to do that for yourself. And so do I.

Every Sunday, when I'm coming home from preaching, I peek outside the plane to see if I catch a baggage handler mistreating my suitcases. (Them jokers ripped my suitcase once!) Before the plane is parked, I see a ramp agent with a pair of these orange wands, kind of steering the pilot where to park and when to stop.

My brother, who works at the airport, tells me that he has heard of times when the pilot is just simply defiant and does not pay his navigator any mind. When this happens, the procedure for the ramp agent is to drop the two wands on the floor and walk away. If something happens, it will not be because of a lack of warning or instructions; it'll be because of pilot stubbornness or refusal to take heed.

I can picture God in heaven warning us the same way.

With two orange wands, He's telling us what we should do and when to stop. Let's let Him. We don't want God to drop His pair of orange wands and walk away, do we? It can happen. In fact, it has happened. Remember the story of Samson[3] or King Saul?[4]

Why not start getting ready now? Stop playing Mafia Wars on Facebook and start reading and praying more, as I suggested in my "6 Stepz 2 Christ" chapter.

After ministering to a death-row inmate in New Mexico, I said my goodbyes and assured him that I was going to be praying for all the prisoners. As I shook his hand from a slot on the door where he received his meals, he grabbed mine tightly. He said, "What did you call me? A prisoner?" I saw him kind of disturbed and said, "My bad. Is the correct word 'inmate'?"

"No. You called me a prisoner," he said, as I tried to get the guard's attention with my feet. (I looked like I was playing charades with that whole "I got joy like a fountain" song!) "I have given my life to Jesus here, in a jail cell. I am a convicted murderer, but I will go to heaven when Christ comes. Sometimes, I read and pray like fifteen hours a day. But you? I bet you're too busy traveling. And you gotta go to work, huh? You have to go to school and study for your tests. You have to watch your favorite shows on TV and go to the stores and have to take your kid to soccer practice. If you're lucky—only if you're lucky—at the end of the night when you're done with your busy day, you sit and read the Bible or pray for only two minutes a day! You guys are prisoners, even in your freedom. Now I'm wondering who is the prisoner, Mr. Preacher-man, me or you?"

Wow. At first I got mad. "My son don't even play soccer!" But then I thought, *Man, this inmate has just called me a prisoner in the midst of my freedom.* Sadly, he is right. We don't take advantage of the freedom God has given us through His Son, Jesus Christ.

We have that whole "I'll do it tomorrow" attitude. But tomorrow is not promised to any of us. I hear that before Tupac died, Evander Holyfield invited him to accept God as Savior, but he never did. Big Pun was about to get help and start a diet before his massive heart attack at the age of twenty-eight. And Michael Jackson was planning a comeback tour when he died. Tomorrow never came.

I remember watching a play called *Annie* back in elementary school. Some of you guys might remember it as well. It was about a little orphan girl with a red afro. She looked like a white Jackson 5 member! (Come to think about it, I don't know why she was an orphan! Who else has a red afro other than her? There's only one man that has a red afro in this world! Ronald McDonald! Somebody needs to check his DNA. He's trying to hide behind some clown makeup and big red shoes! Somebody should get him to do a blood test on the *Maury Show*! And somewhere in that whole mix, comedian Carrot Top is involved as well! We should get to the bottom of this, fast! Maybe I should blackmail McDonald's, and get free Big Macs for the rest of my life! That'll be awesome!)

Anyways, *Annie* had two songs that were real popular. One of them was "It's the Hard-Knock Life." That was made even more popular by rapper Jay-Z when he did a re-mix to it. The other song I personally hated, but I couldn't get it out of my head. (Auugghh! I hate when that happens!) It was called "Tomorrow." It says "Tomorrow! Tomorrow! I love ya Tomorrow! You're always a day a way." That song is WHACK! We're not promised tomorrow! I want to pull her little red hair and tell her, "Who told you that, you little liar!?" That's antibiblical. The Bible tells me the opposite. It tells me:

- "TODAY, if you hear his voice, do not harden your hearts"![5]
- "NOW is the day of salvation"![6]
- It also says that we don't know what will happen tomorrow.[7]

And, it even warns us in Ephesians: "Watch your step. Use your head. Make the most of every chance you get."[8] So let's start getting our house in order today. Now, while we still got a chance.

Even Apollo Creed yelled at Rocky when Sly told him he was kind of feeling discouraged, but would do better the next day: "THERE IS NO TOMORROW! THERE IS NO TOMORROW! THERE IS NO TOMORROW!"

What if it never comes? What if you don't get that chance to say sorry? What if you never get the opportunity to say I love you, again? Most importantly, what if you never get to ask Jesus to forgive you?

Back in the day, preachers like John the Baptist were straight to the point. He's quoted saying, "Repent, for the kingdom of heaven is near."[9] And Jesus said exactly the same thing.[10] So I want to end this book by telling you the same thing, and leaving you with this question so that you can answer it yourself:

"What shall I do, then, with Jesus who is called Christ?"

1. Matthew 27:22.
2. Philippians 1:21.
3. Judges 16:20.
4. 1 Samuel 28:6.
5. Hebrews 3:7, 8; emphasis added.
6. 2 Corinthians 6:2; emphasis added.
7. James 4:14.
8. Ephesians 5:15, 16, *The Message.*
9. Matthew 3:2.
10. Matthew 4:17.

GLOSSARY

Arroz con gandules: Rice and pigeon peas.

Barrio: Neighborhood.

Bebe kids: Brats.

Beemer: BMW.

Bendito or dito: It's like saying, "Awwww . . ." Feeling sorry.

Bodega: Corner store.

Chancleta/Chanclas: Slippers.

Cheddar: Money.

Chuletas: Pork chops.

Cochina: Dirty. A gross girl.

Coquís: A little Puerto Rican frog that comes out at night to sing.

Crack: Make fun of.

Crib: House. Or apartment. A place where you live.

Cuz: Cousin. Friend. Brother. Or homie.

GLOSSARY

DL: Down low or a secret.

Forty: Forty-ounce bottle of beer.

Gangsta: Gangster.

Grub on: Eat.

Holla at your boy: Call me.

Homeboy or Homie: A good friend.

Hooptie: A beat-up car.

Jabroni: A nerd. A dummy.

Jack: Steal.

La Junta: Church board.

Moms: Mother.

Nada: Nothing.

New jack: A rookie.

Pops: Father.

Props: Respect.

Psych: Just kidding.

Rat: A snitch.

Rebound: "Catch you later."

Reprende a Satanás: Rebuke Satan.

Set tripping: Claiming a gang.

Wild out: Go crazy.

Are you living in the real world?

- Is all this talk about a sugar-coated good life getting on your last nerve?
- Have you felt like Christianity is not your thing?
- Then "Changed" is the book you've been waiting for!

Three ways to order:

1. Local | Adventist Book Center®
2. Call | 1-800-765-6955
3. Shop | AdventistBookCenter.com

Changed is a book about cold, hard realities. It is not a work of fiction, because hearsay is not allowed in the court of life. Eleven writers, including Willy Ramos, testify about their lives and their truths; their messes and their messages. They've been there and done that; they have cried and they have laughed; and they have shouted in desperation towards heaven, searching for answers. Read their stories and find out why it makes so much sense to give Jesus a try.

0-8163-9322-2